D0772362

ב"ה

RAV DOVBER PINSON

THE GARDEN OF PARADOX

THE ESSENCE OF NON DUAL KABBALAH
IN THREE CONVERSATIONS

 IYYUN PUBLISHING

Published by IYYUN Publishing
232 Bergen Street
Brooklyn, NY 11217

http:/www.IYYUN.com

Iyyun Publishing books may be purchased for educational, business or sales promotional use. For information please contact: contact@IYYUN.com

cover and book design: Rochie Pinson

pb ISBN 978-0-9852011-3-5

Pinson, DovBer 1971-
Garden of Paradox: The Essence of Non Dual Kabbalah, in Three Conversations /
DovBer Pinson
1. Judaism 2. Spirituality 3. Philosophy

—IN DEDICATION—

to the

Opaline Fund
of the Jewish Community Federation
and Endowment Fund

and to

MR. JORIAN YONAH SCHUTZ
התמים יונה שיחי׳

May he be blessed to rise higher
and delve deeper and to do so always
from a place of inner joy and clarity.

ACKNOWLEDGMENTS

To the developmental editor of this text
a dear student
Reb Mattisyahu Yisrael Brown שיח'
with gratitude

Many thanks to
Reb Eden Pearlstein שיח'
for his creative input

IN GRATITUDE

NEIL (NACHUM) SIMCES שיח'

AND

STEVEN (MOSHE) HAZAN שיח'

May they experience a Shefa of Beracha
Gashmi and Ruchni

TABLE OF CONTENTS

FOREWORD

回

FOLLOWING THE RIVER
BACK TO ITS SOURCE

FOREWORD

FOLLOWING THE RIVER
BACK TO ITS SOURCE

" G-d planted a Garden in Eden… and placed there the human… G-d made grow out of the ground every tree that is pleasant to look at and good to eat, [including] the Tree of Life in the middle of the garden, and the Tree of Knowledge of good and evil. A river flowed out of Eden to water the garden. From there it divided into four major rivers. "
(Genesis, 2:8-10)

WE LIVE IN A CONFUSED AND CONFUSING WORLD. Everything appears to be at odds with everything else. There is an apparent war between science and faith, money and morals, nationalism and nihilism, love and fear. In such a climate people naturally feel lost and disoriented. This results most frequently in people shutting down and closing themselves off from the immensity and immediacy of the cosmos and all it contains. Bumper stickers, pithy slogans, narrow causes, and free rides to enlightenment have become our culture's common currency.

It is in such a climate that Kabbalah has emerged from the secret vaults of esoteric tradition. Kabbalah has been revealed to and embraced by the masses searching for spiritual substance and sustenance in an unparalleled age of emptiness, where image is everything.

Indeed, the time is right for this secret wisdom to be released to the world. This is due for a variety of reasons including the drastic moral decline that accompanied the exponential growth of industry and technology, as well as various meta-historical calculations that indicate an impending large-scale shift in human consciousness.

This unveiling of the mystical has had a number of positive, as well as negative, effects in the world and in people's lives. For many, it has brought a renewed sense of self and purpose, for others it has been the bridge of return, reconnecting them to their once abandoned tradition, as well as halping to keep the tradition itself viable and relevant in rapidly shifting times.

Alongside the benefits, there has been a shadow side accompanying the unparalledled influx of light. Many of these teachings have been perverted and mass-produced for the financial gain of a select few. Once powerful tools of liberation have been employed to further sedate and hypnotize people into deeper and more dangerous levels of servitude — more dangerous, because they are deceptively couched in the language of liberation. Infatuation with the shimmering surfaces and exotic trappings of these ancient teachings have ensnared hosts of contemporary people within their net of endless products, foreign vocabularies, and abstruse technicalities that all prove meaningless, or worse, if not connected to their vital Source.

It is specifically this dynamic that the book you hold in your hands, Garden of Paradox, seeks to address. Too often people chase after easy answers for instant gratification, obscure details to bolster their fragile ego, or insider information to feel superior. These are all thorns on the Rose of Kabbalah, these are the garments that cover the body that houses the soul that is connected to the Source of All Life and Light.

From our normative perspective, which is defined by the Tree of Knowledge, the world, with all its craziness appears to be a Garden of Paradox. But it is our sincerest prayer that through the process outlined in these pages of following "the river that waters the garden" all the way back to its source, that we may put the fruit back onto the Tree of Knowledge, sit within the shade of the Tree of Life, and return to the Garden of Paradise.

This book attempts to strip away the outer layers of Kabbalah that most often conceal the core teachings. Much like a seed before sprouting must shed its outer shell in order to liberate the latent life energy, we too will discard many of the details and technicalities of Kabbalah in our quest to uncover its vital energy — the seed of the Tree of Life within each and every one of us and within all of creation.

An endeavor such as this, can be tedious and overwhelming. It comes with many questions, doubts, and challenges.

For this reason, the bulk of this information presented here is in the form of real-time dialogues, as conversations and exchanges that serve to highlight this Essential level of Kabbalah.

PART ONE:

OPENING THE TEACHINGS OF KABBALAH

WHAT IS KABBALAH?

THE WORD KABBALAH MAY CONJURE UP images of esoteric charts and elaborate maps of ethereal worlds, sacred names and states of consciousness, numeric-linguistic gymnastics reserved for a spiritual elite, or magical techniques for manipulating reality. While these may in fact be some of the garments of Kabbalah, our exploration will begin with an attempt to understand its essence.

From an academic standpoint, Kabbalah can be viewed as a systematic body of spiritual wisdom with various approaches including:

1] *Theoretical* Kabbalah, primarily concerning itself with the use and interpretation of various symbols and stories as they relate to cosmology.

2] *Meditative* Kabbalah, consisting of rigorous practices and programs of spiritual training for the attainment of expanded, altered, or prophetic states of consciousness.

3] *Magical* Kabbalah, comprised of various techniques and tools, such as amulets and intonations, intended to exert tangible influence upon physical reality.

4] *Personal* Kabbalah, inwardly concentrating the teachings in order to apply them to one's own personal psycho-spiritual development.

From a technical standpoint, we could delve into all the various details of Kabbalah, with the metaphors and vessels that are used to contain and transmit this wisdom or light.

We would begin by introducing the ten Sefirot — the lenses, or prisms, that reflect and refract the light of the Infinite One, causing it to appear as finite form. We could then elaborate on the four fundamental worlds of consciousness, each one contained within the other. We could then create a detailed map of the entire structure and process of creation, from the primordial Infinite Light all the way down to the dense matter of the finite world. This mapping of the Kabbalistic cosmology has been detailed in a previous text entitled, "Thirty-Two Gates of Wisdom: Awakening through Kabbalah". Our quest presently is to attempt to answer a far more elementary, but no less important, set of questions: *What is the inner purpose and essence of Kabbalah? And what is the direct experience of the Kabbalist?"*

FRAGMENTED REALITY

Since the beginning of recorded philosophy there has always been an intuition that all is not only as it seems on the surface — that there is both reality as we see it and reality as it is. Whether it was water that was seen as the underlying elemental reality, or fire, a 'world of appearance' or a 'world of forms', a phenomenal or noumenal world, as the ancient philosophers suggest, distinctions were always made between what we see and what truly is.

Kabbalah is concerned with precisely this sense of separation, this deep wound of dichotomy that we all carry within us. According to the Kabbalistic understanding of the creation story in the Torah, all of humanity has been thrust from a primordial and pristine reality into a fractured world at odds with itself, where we all sense some strange and subtle conflict between reality as it is perceived and reality as it truly is.

This fundamental disconnect pervades all of our perceptions and relationships, whether it is a schizophrenic split within ourselves, societal conflict between us and others, or spiritual distance between us and our Creator. Each of us has at times experienced discrepancies between our authentic inner self and the external image we present to others — the way we feel inwardly and the way we project outwardly. Often we act as though other people, and even the environment, are separate and potentially against us.

Theologically speaking, most of us surmise that somehow the Source of All Reality, the very core of our being, is far-removed and distant from our individual experience. This gives rise to a common belief that there is a Creator somewhere out there, while Creation remains perpetually right here — and never the twain shall meet. This sense of separation pervades all aspects of reality, leaving us with a vague and gnawing sense of distance between us, our deepest selves, others, and our Creator.

THE DESIRE FOR UNIFICATION

Even though we may live this way day to day, there is something deep within us that relentlessly yearns for and aspires towards connectivity and unification. Subconsciously we orient toward wholeness. Even if it is evasive or latent, on some level deep down we can glimpse what is behind the nihilistic mirror of subjective self-projection. This subtle recognition creates a desire, albeit one with a sense of trepidation, to attempt to pierce through the veils and experience that which is beyond the surface appearance of separation.

The desire to reconnect is the primary motivating force behind every activity of all beings. The eternal quest for philosophical or psychological insight, the creative impulse to develop natural sciences, the human desire to love and be loved, all are expressions of a deep longing to bring two back into one.

Due to the perceived reality that we are not yet there, and being that we still see ourselves as living in a fragmented reality of separation, there is a paradoxical counter-tendency. As we all subconsciously seek unification, we are most often scared and insecure. As a result, we often end up looking elsewhere to solve the most important riddles of our own lives.

Following after this reasoning, human intrigue inclines toward objects or issues that are remote, foreign, or novel. For example, people are less likely to fall in love with someone they have known their whole life than with someone they perceive to be exotic or unlike themselves. Similarly, instead of looking deeply into our own lives here and now, we often attempt to explore other people's lives, or other seemingly more exciting topics. Whether it is impulsiveness or ignorance, we somehow find a way to place ourselves outside of the consciousness of unity.

BRINGING THE MIND HOME

At its inception, western science focused on the most remote layers of our world: the stars, planets, and other celestial bodies. Gradually studies of plants, animals, and then humans developed. Astronomy was introduced as the first science and only much later on did anthropology come along. It is not until relatively recently that psychology as we know it, appeared at the end of the 19th century. And now with the emergence of some of the more philosophical leaning quantum physicists, at last science finally seems to be ready to explore the nature of consciousness itself.

The questions intensify as the central range of the human sphere is approached: Why am I here at all? What is my purpose? How can I become aware of my deepest self? How does my consciousness function? Is there a reason for existence? Who am I?

In order to satisfy this level of inquiry we can no longer depend upon external data. We need a science that reveals what the outwardly focused mind cannot see. This is the purpose of the spiritual wisdom of Kabbalah. Through the active engagement and application of creative and contemplative consciousness, the Kabbalist penetrates into the core of the multi-dimensional diamond-in-the-rough of reality in order to experientially understand that there is no separation, no duality, no dichotomy, no conflict between outside and inside; there is only One.

But despite popular misconception, Kabbalah is not a mystical brand of thought. Mysticism implies the fallacy of our empirical perception and sensory experience. Kabbalah, on the other hand, asks us to integrate and elevate our senses. We should not discount what we see, but we should also open up our inner eyes to perceive that which we do not see. Kabbalah urges us to listen close enough to hear what does not make a sound.

THREE FACETED GEM

Within the state of unity, of non-separation, there are no words. There is no need to communicate, so there is no dialogue. There is not even any projection to reflect back in upon itself. You cannot see or observe unity, you can only be it.

In order to teach the concept of unity, the masters of Kabbalah realized that some provisional distance is necessary so that the integral state of wholeness might be apprehended as if from outside. In this way, beings who are suffering from the mistaken belief that they are on the outside may gain access to the inner chambers in order to come closer to the Creator, to themselves, and to each other.

When one emerges, even slightly, from being totally absorbed in unity, three fundamental facets of the kaleidoscopic reality come into view:

1. Elokut — Divinity
2. Olamot — Worlds
3. Neshamot — Souls

These three concepts parallels:
1) Creator
2) Creation
3) Consciousness.

Again, these three are all really One. We cannot think of the Creator without taking creation into account, as well as the human consciousness that contemplates creation. We cannot approach our own soul, or the soul of the world, without encountering the Divine. Every point of the creative process has within it some aspect of the Creator, Creation, and Consciousness that come together to comprise its unique conception.

Although in this book we will be treating these perspectives as three separate facets, we must always remain awake and aware of the fact that we are truly contemplating only One Gem.

DIRECT EXPERIENCE

Kabbalah is not a creed to be accepted on blind faith as dogma or merely understood as symbolic and abstract, but is in fact something to be lived and experienced directly. Kabbalah is not grasped by the mind alone but must be contemplated deeply, integrated wholly and lived vibrantly with our entire being.

Attempting to learn Kabbalah without allowing it to enter into and resonate throughout your whole self is like walking hungrily into a restaurant and trying to satisfy the appetite by merely reading the menu. You can sit down, read the menu, and even ask the waiter to explain the specials to you; but if you never place your order, open your mouth, chew your food, and digest your meal you will receive no lasting or vital substance from your experience.

Similarly, if we wish to visit Paris we may buy a comprehensive map of the city and study it with diligence and gusto. But if we never actually go there and walk the streets, we will never truly know Paris.

Kabbalah is the pursuit and practical application of the direct knowledge of life. This is hinted at in the literal translation of the word Kabbalah, 'to receive'. Many scholars interpret this as being indicative of the chain of oral transmission through which the Kabbalistic tradition is passed on. One must receive it from a living teacher; a book is not enough. But there is another dimension to this concept of receiving. This is the ability to be open in order to receive that which is being revealed in the moment. Kabbalah can be understood as the art and science of receptivity — the practical inner wisdom and spiritual technology of becoming receptive.

When we begin to experience and apply Kabbalistic teachings, we find ourselves spontaneously contemplating Divinity. Sensing the Divine presence, or catching a glimpse of it, is so powerful that it illuminates and elevates the way we perceive our physical reality down to the smallest detail. We are now able to sense the spark of Divinity within everything.

Once able to sense Divinity within everything, revealing the inherent inter-connectedness of all life, we begin to experience the world more coherently. It then becomes more and more natural to bring our mind back home, to remain in touch with our deepest self.

With true acceptance and love of self, we begin to see the good qualities in others, and in turn become more compassionate towards all people. Our aptitude to love and our appreciation and respect for all life is immensely enhanced, for we realize that all of life is infused with purpose and destiny. If the world may have seemed cold, indifferent, unfriendly, or accidental — a mere lump of inert matter — we now begin to see that these aspects are merely shells and husks that conceal an Infinite Light. Now we behold that within that shell, there is a Divine animating force, an awareness, an opportunity to elevate.

THREE GATES

THERE ARE NUMEROUS GATES TO ENTER into the experience of Kabbalah. Ultimately they all lead to an immense enrichment of our capacity to live without fear, to appreciate the goodness within all creation, and to be open to love. The powerful teachings of Kabbalah can empower us to truly exercise our freedom to choose to co-create our life.

In this book we will focus on three fundamental approaches to Kabbalah. We will now quickly outline these approaches and the Sages who initiated them in order to further explore the three primary concepts of Creator, Creation, and Consciousness. Keep in mind, it is all One. All three gates lead to the same palace.

ABULAFIA'S GATE:
CONTEMPLATION OF THE CREATOR

Some people are contemplative and ethereal by nature. The spiritual path most appropriate to them might include extensive solitary meditation upon the secrets of Divinity. Rabbi Abraham Abulafia (1240-1296) and his student Rabbi Yoseph Gikatalia (1248-1323) embodied this path. Their meditative teachings revolved around the use of Divine names and their explanations in order to attain prophetic insight and unity with the Creator. The idea of prophecy is to harmonize and align with the Shefa or 'Divine Flow' from the Source of all Intelligence and Abundance. Through advanced visualization and breathing techniques, coupled with the chanting of complex Hebrew letter permutations, the mind, unimpeded by the surface-ego is gradually opened up to this flow of Shefa and ultimately dissolves into a state of effortless unity with the Source of All Life.

LURIA'S GATE:
COSMOLOGY AND CREATION

Other people are primarily scientific or creative. They are curious about how things work. This tendency can manifest itself in art, science, business, politics or any other area of active interest. These people are in some way driven to make the world a better place. The teachings of Rabbi Yitzchak

Luria (1534-1572), known as the Ari or the Arizal, revealed a profound understanding of Creation. His theoretically oriented teachings include the creative process of how the universe comes into being, the inner structure of creation, the explanation for existential anxiety, the pervading sense of cosmic brokenness, and the spiritual potential for repairing the universe known as Tikkun Olam or 'Fixing the World'. Included in these teachings, special attention is also given to the psycho-spiritual process of achieving our own individual Tikkunim or 'Fixings' so that we do not need to experience reincarnation again; or put in more psychological and personal terms, to not have to continuing learning the same lesson over and over again — to evolve.

BAAL SHEM TOV'S GATE:
CONSCIOUSNESS IS THE KEY

A third group of people may be drawn to understanding themselves and others inter- and intra-personally. Their spiritual quest may involve creating conscious community and cultivating selfless love for other people and for all of the Creator's creations. Rabbi Yisrael Ben Eliezer (1698-1760), better known as the Baal Shem Tov, brought the world a new way of joy and love. His personally oriented path of kindness and openness to all, regardless of levels of learning, refinement, status or stature, became a popular revolutionary and revivalist movement known as Chasidism or Hassidism. Unity with the Creator in this path is attained through a profound level of self-understanding, humility, joy, and compassion for all of the Creator's creations. Ac-cording to the Baal Shem Tov, all the theoretical and cos-mological teachings of the Kabbalah are to be applied to each individual's psycho-spiritual development and individ-ual experience. This is achieved through ecstatic prayer, meditation, dance, folk-stories, and most importantly by way of tangible acts of selfless love. According to the original teachings of Chassidism, not only do you meditate on emp-tying yourself of all sense of ego and separateness, you actu-ally live this way in regard to others.

In the following chapters we will follow this historical un-folding of Kabbalistic philosophy and practice. We will take these profound teachers as our guides, enter through their respective gates, and strive to experience their understand-ings of Creator, Creation, and Consciousness.

RECEIVING THE TEACHINGS

Kabbalah literally means 'receiving'. This implies a tradi-tion that was transmitted orally from master to disciple. The nuanced meaning of the word Kabbalah is 'to be open to re-ceive'. We must open ourselves to a wisdom that may be in-consistent with our prior knowledge or paradigm of understanding the world if we are to attempt to absorb a new level of awareness and state of being.

PART TWO:

◙

WHAT DOES NON-DUAL MEAN?

Before we delve too deeply into our topic, as a way of introduction, let us set some basic principles.

THREE PERSPECTIVES

There are three fundamental perceptions or possible perspectives:

1) **Finite Form:** *Yesh* — Something
2) **Infinite Formless:** *Ayin* — Nothing
3) **Beyond & Including All Reality:** *Yesh Amiti* — True Existence

1: FINITE FORM

The first level of perception is one that is gained through our senses. In this realm of perception we experience and observe reality through a series of dualities and dichotomies such as inside/outside, up/down, right/left, black/white, past/future, me/you, and subject/object. This is the reality of perception via our senses. This is the world of form and movement. The Hebrew word for this realm is Yesh. Yesh represents Some-thing-ness, existence, the manifest.

2: INFINITE FORMLESS

The second level of perception is one of non-duality, where we sense only unity. From this perspective there is a complete collapse of the two into one. There is no longer an inside and an outside, object and subject, up and down, past and future, me and you. All is now perceived as one seamless whole, beyond time, space, and all forms of separation and movement. The Hebrew word for this is Ayin or No-thing-ness, emptiness — the Non-Dual.

3: BEYOND & INCLUDING ALL REALITY

The third and deepest level of perception is one that is beyond form and non-form, the Ultimate that transcends and includes both manifestation and non-manifestation, movement and stillness. The word for this in Hebrew is Yesh Amiti, 'True Existence'. Succinctly put, G-d is found within everything, and there is nothing besides G-d. Not that all reality is G-d, but rather that all of reality is part of G-d.

Another way of understanding these three states:

1) On the Yesh level the world Exists (i.e. the word is seen as being real).
2) On the Ayin level the world does Not Exist (i.e. the world is seen as being an illusion).
3) On the Yesh Amiti level the world both exists and does not exist, and neither exists nor does not exist.

THREE NAMES

These three perspectives are related to three "Names" of G-d as described in the Torah:

1) Elokim (אלקים) — Divine Force manifest within Nature *
2) Hashem (י-ה-ו-ה) — Infinite, Transcendent Unity, Beyond Nature
3) Ani (אני), or Anochi (אנכי) — I Am, Essence, beyond beyond, within within, beyond within, within beyond

---

* This name is plural and, as such, is a reference to the hiding of the One within the many. The account of Creation in the Torah uses this name to acknowledge the Divine Attribute of the creative process. Also, the spelling of the name is intentionally obscured in this text.

To further illustrate this association of the three states of consciousness and the three Divine Names let's take an example found in the text of the Torah.

This particular passage describes an event during one of Moshe's first encounters with the Divine: "Elokim (אלקים) spoke to Moshe, and said to him, "Ani (אני) Hashem (י-ה-ו-ה)" *(Exodus, 6:2)*.

In this one verse there is Ani (אני), there is Elokim (אלקים), and there is Hashem (י-ה-ו-ה).

Elokim is expressing to Moshe that there is only One (Hashem), and that One is the Ultimate 'I AM' of Ani.

In order for us to understand even a sliver of this seemingly simple sentence, let us take a closer look beneath the surface of these particular Names.

Elokim (אלקים) is connected with nature, creation, multiplicity, and time-space consciousness. In the Torah it is Elokim who creates the Heavens and the Earth. The Hebrew word for nature, *Ha'Teva*, has the same numerical value as the name Elokim: 86. Elokim is associated with the attribute of *Din*, Judgment. This quality manifests within the Laws of Nature such as gravity and the cycles of life. Natural Laws are universal, indifferent, and unapproachable by

---

It is a tradition not to pronounce certain Divine Names outside of the context of Torah and Prayer. (the 'k' is really an 'h', and the 'ק' is really a 'ה')

humans seeking respite from their tyranny. If you touch fire, you get burned. If you are underwater too long, you drown. Elokim is plural indicating that it is through the creative process that multiplicity, as experienced in nature, is brought into reality. Elokim is the Divine Immanent, the aspect of the One that is always present within the many.

Hashem (ה–ו–ה–י) represents the Infinite aspect of G-d that is beyond nature. The four letters that comprise this Name, when rearranged, can spell the Hebrew words for past (היה), present (הוה), and future (יהיה), indicating that this name transcends all concepts of time. Hashem is associated with the attribute of Mercy. It is to Hashem that one directs their prayers for healing, salvation, help, or miraculous intervention. Hashem is understood as the Infinite aspect of G-d, but also paradoxically represents an approachable aspect of infinity. If nature is cold and indifferent to suffering, Hashem is personal and compassionate.

Ani (אני), the third reality, is the 'I am' of G-d, so to speak. This is the unity between Elokim and Hashem, between nature and miracle, between time and eternity, between me and You — leaving only us, only One, only I, Ani. Not much can be said about Ani. Ani simply is — beyond distinction, description, or direction. It is to Ani that the psalmist directs the words "To You silence is praise". No description is sufficient because any attempt to describe Ani, even just saying Infinity, is, by definition, a limitation.

Ultimately, Ani is the equanimous backdrop, or fertile ground of being, upon which the dynamic interplay between Elokim (Nature) and Hashem (Spirit) manifests as reality, dream, existence or illusion — depending upon your perspective. But the main point is that Ani is both beyond and within all Names or attributes. Ani is transcendent as well as immanent, and also neither.

THREE PATHS

Experientially, these three paradigms are experienced as:

1) **Bitul Ha'Yesh** — Humbling the Ego

2) **Bitul Ha'Metziyut** —Nullification of Ego

3) **B'Chol Le'Vavcha** — With all your Hearts; Transparency of Ego

1. BITUL HA'YESH, (I)

This is the spiritual work of aspiring to humble the ego, otherwise known as the path of humility. During this point of the process, the small i exists, yet one is working on refining it. The small i, or ego, can be compared to Pharaoh from the book of *Shemot* or Exodus: a vital and important aspect of a whole system which has fanatically seized control and seeks to project itself as the only valid authority.

The work of Bitul ha'Yesh is to empower one's Soul to
"speak truth to power" like Moshe did to Pharaoh. This
initiates the attempt to liberate one's life from the tyran-
nical grip of the over-inflated ego.

At this stage, one is still functioning from a self-centered
paradigm.

2. BITUL HA'METZIYUT, (You)

This is the spiritual work of totally nullifying one's ego.
The goal of this work is for a person to function from a
place of non-attachment and equanimity. From this perspective all stimulus, sensation, and scenario is seen as illusory and ultimately non-existent. Following the
previously mentioned metaphor of the Exodus, this
process can be compared to the Israelites leaving Egypt
and entering into the wilderness. Psychologically speaking
this is the process of deconditioning and deconstruction
that is necessary to consciously recreate one's own identity.
This stage can be compared to a cosmic reset button. The
small i ceases to exist. It is a paradigm of only You, as i no
longer exist, so to speak.

3. B'CHOL LE'VAVCHA, (I and I)

This phrase literally translates as, "with all your hearts".
This implies an integrated state of being in which both
the I and the You are activated and acknowledged within

a rectified consciousness, a transparency of ego. This refers to a state of consciousness in which both one's creative and destructive impulses are enlisted in the spiritual efforts of an individual. Both one's selfish, survival instinct as well as one's selfless, spiritual intuition are united in the perpetual process of Deveikut, 'Cleaving to the Divine', and Tikkun, 'Fixing or Repair' of all that is broken or needs healing. From this perspective life is both Real and a Dream. Everything depends on one's freewill, and it is all up to G-d. This requires an integration of one's ego as well as their transcendent Self. The ego still exists, but it becomes transparent to one's inherent transcendence. This is a paradigm of you and me; a recognition that we are all manifestations of the Ultimate I.

THREE WAYS TO RELATE

These three principles also illustrate our relationship with our Creator.

1) **I-You:** *Love*
2) **I-It:** *Awe*
3) **I-I:** *Unification*

1) The first level is **love**. When one is in love, they feel themselves to be subsumed by something that is greater than themselves, but there is still a pronounced experience of the I. There is an I that loves. Implicit in the statement, "I love You", is that there is a strong sense of I consciousness. There

is an I that is in love. When we are in love with, and feel loved by, the Creator we feel close, connected, and cradled. Yet, there is a clear me and a clear You, and I love You.

2) The second level in relationship with our Creator is **awe**. Awe is the evolution of love, which is an emotion that is ordinarily dependent upon some form of conditionality (i.e. what You do for Me). Awe manifests primarily as an experience of intoxicated appreciation for the Other in and of Itself. While we behold our Beloved in awe, our relationship becomes one of transcendence. Instead of an emotional experience that anchors one in their sense of self, awe is a form of love that liberates one from oneself. Awe is that overwhelming sensation of the majesty, wonder, and amazement at creation, matched with a humble recognition of our existential smallness within the vastness of all creation and it's Creator. An 'Aha! Moment', or a Peak Experience, signals the total (but often temporary) disappearance of the small I. There is a total collapse of the small-self and ego. We are completely absorbed by the Other. The possibility of wonder and radical amazement is present when we stand in awe before the mystery of all creation and the Creator. The Holy Other is Infinitely beyond me, a mystery — an It.

3) The third level transcends relationships altogether. Relationships, by definition, suggest duality and separation. Love and awe are both feelings. Feelings either draw us closer, as in love, or force us to stand back, as in awe. Yesh

Amiti is beyond these conditional dynamics. Yet, at this integral level, Yesh Amiti, also includes all relationships and emotions, including love and awe. The Reality of Unity is where the small i becomes a conscious and co-creative reflection of the Ultimate I.

After Adam and Eve ate from the Tree of Knowledge of Good and Evil — the Tree of Duality — they were exiled from the Garden of Eden, a paradigm of Unity. In the Torah's description, following this episode, the verse states that the Creator "stationed two Cherubim east of the Garden of Eden, each with a revolving fiery sword, to guard the way to the Tree of Life" *(Genesis, 3:22-24)*. The function of the Cherubim is to guard the path that leads to the Tree of Life. They are stationed at the gates of the Garden of Eden in order to intimidate us and scare us away from embarking upon such a spiritual journey. Paradoxically, the word Cherubim comes from the same root as *Kiruv*, To bring close. The two Cherubim and their fiery swords are there to both repel and attract us to a more holistic and holy way of being in the world.

The two Cherubim represent Love and Awe. Indeed it is the elemental emotions of Love and Awe that propel us all the way up to the gates of the Garden of Eden. And yet to pass through the final gate in order to gain entry into a state of unity, all emotions must be made transparent, surrendered, transcended, and on the deepest level, integrated within one's fully realized self.

THREE AVENUES OF ACTION

These three paradigms are also reflected in one's experience of interpersonal relationships and exchanges between people. Take for example the act of a person reaching out to help someone else.

1) "I am doing you a favor": *Me*

2) "It's not about me but about You": *You*

3) "We are all One": *Us*

1: ME

From the first perspective — a self-centered approach to social activism — when a person helps someone else, doing them a favor for example, both the giver and the receiver are very much aware that the giver is doing a favor for the recipient out of the goodness of their heart. Both the giver and receiver are acutely aware of their separation. The roles of giver as giver and receiver as receiver are unquestioningly maintained. If you walk down the street and blindly drop a dollar into a cup without looking into that person's eyes or at least smiling, then it is clear that you and the beggar are separate. The resultant message is that you, because of your own generosity, are giving to them.

2: YOU

In the second perspective — the Other-Centered approach to social activism — your consciousness is more evolved. When you see someone in need, you really see them; you empathize, sympathize, and feel their pain. And so, when you see someone less fortunate than you, the knee jerk reaction that tells you to "horde your money for yourself" is nullified in that moment. The emphasis is no longer on you, but becomes about the other in need. You put yourself aside for the needs of an 'other'.

3: US

The third perspective is the awareness that we are all expressions of the Creator's unity and that it is not only about me, or you, but about us. We are all here for a purpose. The fact that you have more and another person has less is by the Creator's design so that you can learn the art of giving and they can learn the art of receiving, or vice versa. In this way, paradoxically, helping someone else is really helping yourself. When action springs from within this place of unity, you are no longer merely doing someone a favor by giving charity or otherwise helping them out, although of course you are doing that as well; nor are you simply feeling their pain, but truly all existence emerges as inter-dependent. Everyone plays a vital role in the fulfillment of some greater purpose that both transcends and includes all of our personal paths.

On this unitive level of awareness there is no collapsing of individuality and distinction within the infinite Other. Our personal I returns as a reflection of the Ultimate I. We are all One, but we are not all the same. The absolute truth of impersonal reality is only valid on the second level of perception, where all is only Infinite Emptiness and No-Thing-Ness. But neither are we totally separate from the rest of creation. That truth is only valid from the lowest perception of the finite ego contained solely in the physical body.

Ultimately, we are all inter-connected individuals. Each one of us is born for both a collective and a specific purpose. We have genetics and spiritual qualities that are the same, and we have genetics and spiritual qualities that are different. Different is not better or worse, just different. We would all do well to respectfully celebrate and share our differences, distinctions, and individualities. This must occur not from a place of privilege and hierarchy, but from an active acknowledgment of the universal archetype of uniqueness and individuation coupled with a strong sense of shared destiny.

So from the deepest perspective, all these vantage points are valid and should be valued, for truly we do have an ego, and yet, we are also transcendent of that ego. The harmony between these two apparently divergent perspectives is to recognize that differences do not equal separation. All small 'i's' are expressions of the One Ultimate I of the Creator.

TO SUMMARIZE

1:

The first perspective (Yesh, Elokim, Humility, Love) is a self-centered perspective, where my I is separate from your I. Life is conceived of as a constant struggle between me and you, us and them. It is a perspective of scarcity, limitation, definition, physicality, and multiplicity. Ultimately, it is a paradigm based upon that which separates us.

2:

The second perspective (Ayin, Hashem, Nullification, Awe) is a soul-centered perspective. From this vantage point one approaches life with the constant awareness that we are all infinite souls vested within finite bodies. According to this paradigm it is our soul, our light, our unity, our collectivity, our underlying universal connection that is important. There is no longer any me or you, just us, only unity; all is one. This is the classic definition of non-duality.

3:

The deepest perspective (Yesh Amiti, Ani, Transparency, Unification) is the reemergence of individuality within the context of unity. This is a non-duality that includes multiplicity, the universal that includes the unique, a spirituality that includes physicality. From this place we are blessed with the Ultimate Awareness that all finite expressions of self are truly emanations of the Essence, of Ani. "Adam Olam Katan, Olam Adam Gadol", Every Human Being is a small World, and the World is a big Human Being. We are but the particulars of Infinity.

1) Individuality *(Unique)*
2) Collectivity *(Universal)*
3) Individuality within the Collective
   (Unique within the Universal)

1) Body
2) Soul
3) Unity of Body & Soul

In the following chapters we will delve more deeply into these details, but this foundation is important before we venture any further.

THREE PARADIGMS & THEIR PERCEPTUAL POINTS OF REFERENCE

	YESH *Something*	AYIN *Nothing*	YESH AMITI *Essence*
REALITY	The world exists	The world does not exist	The world both exists & does not exist
BEING	Finite Form	Infinite Formless	Beyond & Including all Form and Formlessness
EXISTENTIAL ORIENTATION	Individual/ Unique	Collective/ Universal	Individual within collective/ Unique within Universal
G-D NAME	Elokim אלקים	Hashem י–ה–ו–ה	Ani אני
SELF IDENTIFICATION	Body	Soul	Unity of Body and Soul
SPRITUAL PRACTICE	Bitul Ha'Yesh/ Humble the Ego	Bitul Ha'Metziut/ Nullify the Ego	B'Chol L'vavcha/ With all your Hearts
RELATIONSHIP	I+You=Love	I+It=Awe/Fear	I+I=Unification
INTERACTION	I am doing you a favor	You are suffering and I can help	We are all One

PART THREE:

THREE CONVERSATIONS;
CREATOR, CREATION & CONSCIOUSNESS

THREE CONVERSATIONS:
A PREFACE

Overall, it can be posited that many people's questions, and even personalities, fall within three archetypal perspectives:

THE PHILOSOPHER,
primarily concerned with an understanding
of concepts within a developed context;

THE ACTIVIST,
committed to putting any
teachings into tangible practices toward the
'Healing of the World';

THE MYSTIC,
magnetically pulled in the direction of navigating their
own internal universe wherein they find the key to unlock
the hidden treasuries of creation.

In the three conversations that follow:
Student 1 is the Philosopher
Student 2 is the Activist
and **Student 3 is the Mystic.**

The three students presented within the course of these conversations provide a voice for each of these three perspectives.

CONVERSATION ONE:

CREATOR

CONVERSATION ONE:
CREATOR

Several students are gathered around their teacher's table singing a Niggun or 'wordless melody' most often used for meditation. As the voices get stronger, the atmosphere changes. The song speaks to their souls, the sound creates a surrounding field. Slowly, the melody begins to fade and fall away. Silence settles in and there is a sense of stillness.

TEACHER: Tonight we are going to explore the concept of "knowing G-d". This is a common phrase, found in the Torah, and used by the early Kabbalists to describe the nature of their spiritual quest. Before we begin, I am interested to know if there are any initial questions or concerns about this phrase? What first comes to your mind when you hear the phrase, "to know G-d"?

STUDENT 1: Well, I don't feel like we can ever really know the nature of the Creator. As I understand it, the Creator is infinite and our minds are finite. It doesn't seem like a realistic possibility.

TEACHER: This is a good point. Our minds seem to be confined by the coordinates of space and time. How are we supposed to understand or connect with something that is not bound by those same parameters? Do we even have a language capable of expressing such a connection if it was attained? Keep these questions in mind as we continue to delve into this conundrum. Anybody else?

STUDENT 2: What I am stuck on is this: What do you really mean when you use the word G-d? I feel like most people just throw this word around as if everyone already understands what it refers to. It seems like something major that we're all just taking for granted. But I for one, would really appreciate it if we could start at the beginning: Who, What, Where, When, Why is G-d?

THE INFINITE

TEACHER: This is an excellent place to begin. Throughout the ages our sages have introduced many different faces of G-d, or aspects of the Divine, as it were. This sounds contradictory because the Torah is always talking about the Ultimate Unity of G-d, but it is also understood that the One Essence has many (apparent) attributes. This is an idea generated from the Torah, which refers to the One G-d by many different names.

There is a meta-logic to this idea. It goes something like this: If we say that G-d is One, but also that the One is Infinite, then it is clear that the One can manifest in many masks — hence the multiple names for One G-d. This alludes to the ancient teaching that we can never know G-d's Essence, but only G-d's attributes. This means that we can never fully understand the absolute mystery of G-d at its innermost core, but we can get a sense of G-d through G-d's actions in the world.

Ultimately we can only know that we don't know. G-D remains an eternal mystery. But we can say that the Torah teaches us that G-d is One, G-d is Unique, and G-d is Infinite. Paradoxically we can also say that the Torah teaches us that G-d created a finite world out of infinity, G-d is aware of each individual creation, and G-d is approachable by humanity. In fact, the Torah even teaches us that G-d desires a relationship with the world. Not only can G-d be approached, but G-d actually wants to be approached.

If this all sounds very paradoxical, that's because it is. But we need to remember that there is something deeper than finite, linear logic. Perceived paradox often leads beyond itself to some form of inconceivable truth. But to approach this truth one must get out of their head and break down some of the mind's walls that keep us contained in our normative consciousness.

STUDENT 2: OK I get it. G-d cannot be defined. I guess I just have to get comfortable with the unknown.

TEACHER : Right. I think that's a good place for us all to start from: The place of openness and unknowing. Once you think you know, you know you don't. But let's take a look at what some of the Kabbalists had to say about this elusive idea of knowing G-d.

In the era of R. Abraham Abulafia and R. Gikatalia, the early period in which Kabbalistic teachings were first written down to be published, the focus of the Kabbalist was to know G-d. When speaking of G-d they would use the term, *"Ohr Ein Sof."* This appellation literally translates as, light without end. This is the Infinite, Formless, Limitless Light. This was the name of choice used by the Kabbalists to describe the Indescribable: The Infinite One.

So the first question has to be: What did they mean by the Infinite? Infinity in terms of the Ohr Ein Sof is not a mathematical infinity, as in an infinite amount of finite stuff. Rather, Ohr Ein Sof is altogether outside of the context of time and space.

When we are told, for example, that a certain galaxy is one hundred billion light-years away this implies that the galaxy is some 588,000,000,000,000,000,000,000 miles away. For those who don't know: Light travels at 186,000 miles per second and a light year is some 5,880,000,000,000 miles. So we can see from these astronomically large numbers that it may seem that this particular galaxy is an infinitely far distance away. But no matter how mind-boggling these numbers are, they are still not in the realm of the Infinite.

True Infinity is utterly discordant to the mathematical, or even the philosophical, interpretation of the infinite, which usually refers to something that is un-measurable and non-dimensional. The Infinite that is implied by the Ohr Ein

Sof is of another order all together and is therefore beyond all imaginable definitions, limitations, or restrictions.

STUDENT I: All right, this is starting to make a little more sense.

TEACHER : Good. Let's go deeper. We also need to understand what the Kabbalists meant by knowing. One of you asked, how is it that an Infinite reality can be known, touched, or even approached by a finite mind? This is a great question. Let's try to answer it.

Our brain is a dualistic and limited operating system that seeks to rationalize and contextualize whatever we perceive from within our senses. We do so based on our prior exposure to stimulus and the ways we may have rationalized similar perceptions at earlier times. This means that what we perceive is a confluence between what is seen and how it is seen. Our own pre-existing internal mental frame of reference gives what we see a classification and context. We require this context or contrast in order to recognize that something actually exists.

This all describes how our minds normally work. But the Kabbalists were not interested in knowledge the way we normally understand it. In their attempts to know G-d, they were not concerned with amassing an inert lump of mere descriptive data. They were attempting to know in the Biblical sense — meaning to unite with in order to achieve some form of intimacy and existential identification. To do this they would utilize various meditative techniques including visualizations, chanting, extreme exegesis, and breathing exercises. Through these experiential approaches to the subject matter they attempted to get beyond the mind in order to encounter the Creator outside of the standard definitions and limitations usually employed by the mind to make sense of stimulus and phenomena. These meditative techniques were an example of the Kabbalists impulse to stop making sense.

STUDENT 3: I can relate to these Kabbalists yearning to know something that is borderless and indefinable. We all seek, on some level, to know what is beyond our perception. But is this really feasible?

STUDENT 2: Part of me thinks that we should not even attempt this, but should just accept our human limits and resign ourselves to more sensible and rational goals, such as living in a way that makes our life meaningful.

STUDENT 1: Or could it be that this very quest — to connect to the Infinite — no matter how impossible it seems, is what gives our finite lives and goals meaning?

TEACHER: These are all the right questions. And I just want to point out that they all bring up different concerns. The first question is ultimately one of technique and functionality when it comes to knowing G-d. The second question is about the overall purpose of such a pursuit. And deeper still, it is a question about the essential purpose of our lives and how we spend our time and energy. The third question seems to be addressing the meaning inherent in such a quest, as well as the overall mechanism of finding meaning in our lives in general.

Without addressing any of these questions directly, I'm going to try to give a more general overview and hope that we touch on some relevant elements of each of these three inquiries. Sometimes an indirect or roundabout route is a more effective way of getting somewhere. Especially when the more direct option is full of overgrowth and obstacles that will only serve to strengthen the resistance to any who seek passage through to the other side of reality as it is already understood. Is that ok?

ALL 3 STUDENTS: Yes. Sounds good. Sure.

TEACHER: Then let's begin.

A natural yearning for the super-natural propelled these Kabbalists into this paradoxical quest. They were totally committed to the dictum of the Torah to 'Know G-d'.

Understanding from the Torah that we could or should know G-d implies that this is somehow possible. But the question still remains: How are we to know the unknowable? What does it mean to know G-d? Where do we learn the 'how' of knowing G-d? The Torah itself gives us the key to unlock this gate: "You must know today, and take it into your heart, that Hashem is Elokim...There is nothing else" *(Deuteronomy, 4:39).*

The name Hashem literally means The Name — the Ineffable Name of the Nameless — that which transcends all definition or description. We pronounce the name Hashem when the Tetragrammaton (י–ה–ו–ה) is written. It is our tradition that we do not pronounce the Tetragrammaton. Some sources say that the exact pronunciation of the four-letter name was lost during our many exiles.

Deeper still, this name may be, by its very nature, unpronounceable. Some esoteric sources claim that this name was never meant to be pronounced in the first place.

This perspective changes the significance of the name. It transforms it from being an essential name of G-d that we have lost or forgotten the correct pronunciation of, to being an ancient linguistic acknowledgment of the limitations of language when it comes to describing the Ultimate Nature of Reality. Its true and ingenious utility may very well lie within the foundation of its un-pronouncability. According to this understanding, those who try to speak the unspeakable are like those who attempt to assign a sound to silence, as if lighting a candle in the daytime would add any more light. They are missing the point of what it means to acknowledge the futility of naming the nameless.

The name Elokim indicates that same Ultimate Reality, but this attribute of the Divine serves as an interface between finite and Infinite. Elokim serves as a bridge across the quantum chasm that divides the Infinite One from Finite Multiplicity. Elokim dims the Infinite light, as it were, so that finite minds can relate to the Infinite Reality through the linguistic medium of definitions and descriptions. Our minds can relate to limited metaphors for the Limitless such as: Personal G-d, Divine Parent, Beloved One, or Creator of the World.

STUDENT 1: That certainly is a paradox: Using a name that implies definition as a bridge to what is un-definable, and maybe even ultimately unbridgeable.

TEACHER: The real problem with using metaphorical definitions such as these is that we run the risk of placing conceptual borders on the Borderless. As soon as we draw borders, we must learn to go beyond them. "Hashem is Elokim" means: Expressions of the Infinite can be found within the finite world. Yet, whenever we find traces of the Infinite, when we sense that there is something beyond ourselves, we are compelled to go beyond even that. But then the verse continues, "there is nothing else."

STUDENT 3: How do we go about finding expressions of the Infinite? And how do we cross those bridges? Is it even possible?

FROM THE FINITE
TOWARDS THE INFINITE

TEACHER: Let's get back to the statement, "There is nothing else". Let's delve into some of the experiential tools that Kabbalah uses to foster Divine consciousness, such as:

1) Cultivating awareness of Divine Providence,

2) Meditating on the Tree of Life,

3) Meditating on Divine Names, and

4) Practicing devotional acts of faith, love and awe.

These tools are themselves creations of the Creator and when used correctly they can lead us along a path towards Divine consciousness, for such is their intended purpose.

The creative process of Kabbalistic consciousness is colorful and replete with elaborate imagery, but its aim is to point to the colorless, imageless, transparent reality of the Ohr Ein Sof Itself.

Let us explore these tools and techniques a bit. But remember, the most important thing is for you to do them on your own. These seeds will not bear fruit unless they are planted, watered, and tended properly.

CONTEMPLATING
DIVINE PROVIDENCE

TEACHER: In order to become aware of Divine Providence or spiritual synchronicity, we can begin by contemplating all the meaningful patterns within creation, within history, and within our own experiences. See if you are able to sense the Divine intelligence orchestrating everything. Even if you do not fully believe this, try to entertain the potential of the perspective. What would the world look or feel like from this vantage point?

For example, perhaps you were thinking of a certain person and spontaneously that person shows up in your life. Or you were thinking about a certain idea and all of a sudden you stumble across a book or teacher who perfectly explains the complexity of the conundrum. The deeper you look, the more you can see that these so-called coincidences are constantly happening and that they only serve to further illustrate the infinitely intelligent, omni-present, orchestrating hand of the Creator. A constant awareness of *Hashgacha Peratit*, Divine Providence, helps us to transform everything that happens in our lives into a kind of mirror, story, or song in which we can perceive, acknowledge, and reflect upon Divine orchestration.

There's also another side to this. Every action we do, whether we are aware of it or not, has an effect on the whole of creation. This is also part of Divine Providence. Every kind word uttered, or loving deed done, introduces positive energy into the universe. For example, it is said that when you speak respectfully to your spouse or partner, that every person, plant, animal, and inanimate object has a greater potential for co-existing harmoniously. In such a way, we are partners with the Creator in the creative process of life as we know it. Our personal actions can affect the cosmic flow of divine energy that streams into and supports creation.

MEDITATION ON DIVINE PROVIDENCE

Before beginning this meditation, make sure that you are in a quiet and comfortable environment where you will not be disturbed or distracted.

Sit comfortably. Feel the ground beneath your feet and the sturdy support of the seat of the chair. As you settle in to yourself, be aware of any relatively pleasant sensation you may have right now. Sense how lucky you are to be here studying.

Think of a good deed that you have done, no matter how small. See the goodness from within that small action rippling out to all of humanity, bringing happiness to many people. Think of how the Divine purpose placed in your mind the impulse to do that deed...

Now think about a time when your life was saved, rescued, or drastically altered for the positive. If nothing comes to mind, contemplate a loved ones story as if it were your own.

See how one event led to another. Connect the seemingly isolated occurrences that eventually resulted in your being 'who' and 'where' you are today. Contemplate the Hashgacha Peratit behind what happened, even if this intelligence seems imperceptibly subtle. Find the part that only an all-knowing Protector could orchestrate including the Hashgacha Peratit that was streaming through your own actions. Stay with this humble miracle for a timeless moment....

When you are ready come back to an awareness of your body, the chair under you, your feet firmly on the floor. As you gradually open your eyes, look around and sense the subtle shift within you. Everything is exactly the same, and yet so very different.

(long silence)

TEACHER: How was your experience?

STUDENT 2: That was very deep. I finally feel like I am starting to understand just a bit more of what the purpose of this kind of work could be. I feel like developing this kind of awareness actually deepens my connection to other beings and makes our sense of shared inter-dependence and reciprocal responsibility even more tangible than it was before. Before this meditation, my desire for social action was much more philosophical and politically based. Now I feel an almost palpable connection to all of creation. Like we really are all one thing or being. Helping others feels so much more natural from this perspective.

SEFIROT – EMANATIONS

TEACHER: Now let's shift back to the mode of intellectual contemplation. While the Ohr Ein Sof is utterly infinite and transcendent of all descriptions, from our perspective the Creator does create and interact with the creation of all living beings. This process occurs through the elaborate symbolic construct of the Kabbalistic Tree of Life, which consists of what are referred to as the ten *Sefirot*.

The Kabbalists use the Tree of Life to describe the creative process. This refers to both the creation of the cosmos as well as to the creativity of human consciousness, from the Infinite One Light to its many manifestations in the finite world.

The Tree of Life is comprised of the ten Sefirot.

The Sefirot are like colored lenses, through which the one clear light of the Infinite contracts itself in order to make room for and manifest the colorful multiplicity of creation. The Sefirot are not separate or independent forces. They are inter-dependent channels through which the Source of All Life — the Creator — animates creation. The Sefirot are the transmitters through which the Infinite Will of the Creator manifests within the world of finite form. These ten cosmic meridians through which the divine energy flows can be called the spiritual DNA or skeletal structure of all of created reality.

The ten Sefirot are:

Keter – Crown, Faith, Will: *Super-Conscious*
Chochmah – Wisdom: *Intuition*
Bina – Understanding: *Reason*
Chesed – Kindness: *Love*
Gevura – Strength: *Restraint*
Tiferet – Beauty: *Compassion*
Netzach – Victory: *Perseverance*
Hod – Acknowledgment: *Humility*
Yesod – Foundation: *Connection*
Malchut – Royalty: *Receptivity*

These ten Sefirot together create a geometric diagram, referred to as the Tree of Life, which provides a meditative guide for journeying upward and inward towards our Infinite Source. But instead of simply analyzing and discussing the intricacies of the Tree of Life, we must climb into it. The more we make the Sefirot real, the more real they become for us.

According to the Kabbalistic conception of meditative prayer, while the inner intention and request is always directed to the One Source of All Life, we may focus as well on one or more of the Sefirot or attributes of the Most High.

This is similar to a citizen who requests of his king to fulfill a need knowing full well that the fulfillment of this need will require the king to command one of his ministers. If, for example, the citizen requests financial help from the king and the king desires to respond to that request by offering some monetary help, the king will then order his royal treasurer to bestow that gift. The essence of the Divine is transcendent and formless, but it is through the Sefirot that the formless is expressed and experienced in form. Yet, the analogy is not precise, for the Creator is both the king and the treasurer — not to mention the treasury itself — there is no other. Always keep this in mind. The story is always bigger than the symbol. G-d is One, beyond all names, metaphors, or masks.

MEDITATION

TEACHER: Next time you pray, meditate on the Sefira or quality that you perceive as being related to your particular prayer. Notice that what you are doing in prayer, by your very intention, and more importantly, by concretizing your thoughts through vocalization and verbalization, is drawing down Divine awareness and spiritual energy into your life and into the world. For example, if we are praying for kindness, we are seeking to stimulate the Sefira of *Chesed* or Loving Kindness. The Infinite answers our prayer by radiating Clear Light through the colored lens of Chesed. In order to fully receive the Divine response of Chesed we must actualize that Sefira within our own lives. We need to envision a change in our lives before that change can actually happen. We can envision and enliven the Sefira of Chesed through intellectual contemplation of what kindness means, through performing acts of kindness, or even literally by dressing in its representative color, which is white.

STUDENT 1: This is very interesting. I feel like this is all actually starting to make a little more sense to me how the Infinite One Light makes the quantum leap into finite forms. The Tree of Life seems to give a peek into the mechanics of this mysterious process. Obviously it's all based on language, metaphor, and symbolism so it's fairly vague and ambiguous. Nevertheless it also seems paradoxically insightful and strangely accurate. I also really love the complementary mirroring of the cosmic creative process with the creative process of an individual as they seek to exercise their own innate potential. It does say in the Torah, if I remember correctly, that humanity was created in the image of G-d. So if G-d is the creator, then we also must have some of this capacity to create.

TEACHER: That's a beautiful insight. And to take it even deeper, I want to point out that the specific G-d name that is referenced in that phrase from the Torah is Elokim. Remember that Elokim is the creative power of the Infinite One. So that just goes to further support your insight.

DEVOTION

TEACHER: Now let's move away from intellectual contemplation and explore the path of devotion. The Infinite One is perceived from our finite human perspective through many metaphorical faces or 'personalities'. These include Father, Mother, Sibling, Friend, and Spouse.

The Biblical book known as The Song of Songs vividly describes the path of a soul ablaze with the passion of a lover for a beloved, a love that is pure and luminous. This fire can give off the smoke of anguish when there is a sense of separation from the Divine Beloved. The unceasing and painful yearning to merge into the Infinite is part of the very nature of our finite existence. Recognizing this yearning is a very powerful way to draw near to our Beloved.

STUDENT 3: So it's good to yearn?

TEACHER: Yes. Our minds may question the efficacy of this path. How can the love of a finite being ever possibly bridge the gulf between them and that which is Infinite? But the Sages of the Talmud offer us a poetic answer to this perceived paradox when the Talmud states that, "Even more than the calf longs for its Mother, the Mother longs for the calf, to give milk". We think of ourselves as the seekers, but ultimately, our Beloved is actually seeking us and drawing us near. In this dualistic and hierarchical paradigm of higher and lower, the higher and lower are both perpetually seeking each other in order to reconnect.

STUDENT 2: That's a beautiful image. I love the idea of a provider desiring to provide even more than the one receiving desires to receive.

STUDENT 3: I actually feel overwhelmed. To meditate on this concept and imagine the Omnipresent One seeking me is incredible and almost unfathomable.

TEACHER: I'm glad you said that because this touches on our next 'tool': the Path of Awe. We can see how even a glimpse of the immeasurable Divine love can be awe-inspiring. Just like we said, spiritual awe can break through our fixed and finite nature — it can literally blow your mind. When residing under the Eagle's Wings, supported by our timeless Rock of Salvation, strengthened by the Shield of Truth, basking in the Living Presence of our majestic Sovereign, The Infinite One, our fragile vessel of self is utterly exposed. Humbled and no longer limited by our ego, we can receive a flash of the Ohr Ein Sof, 'the Infinite Light'. It is a very good sign when love leads to awe.

STUDENT 3: I love love and I am in awe of awe.

DIVINE NAMES

TEACHER: Now let's move on to another one of the great paradoxes: the many names of the One G-d. One of the favored tools of the early Kabbalists was the contemplation of Divine names. The Creator is One Reality, but is expressed and perceived through the diversity of events, attributes, and emotions. This helps us to understand the Torah's use of different 'names' for the Divine Essence.

A person may introduce himself within different social contexts using various names or appellations. Each name reveals a unique facet of his personality, but all the names point to the same person.

R. Gikatalia envisioned the multiplicity of names as a single tree with many branches. The plurality of Divine names is indicated by the word Elokim, which is grammatically plural. Ultimately, all names are different notes in the same song, the many expressions of the One Reality.

A Divine name is a more direct route to Infinity than is a Sefira, just like my name is a more direct route to my identity than is one of my attributes or abilities. A name is personal and unique, while an attribute is more general. If you were to point to my arm and then at my head you would say, "This is your arm, and that is your head." Only when you want to indicate the whole person will you refer to me by name. Anyone can be nice, loving, or compassionate, but only you can be the 'you' to which your name refers.

The Kabbalistic path of Abulafia frequently employs Divine names in the quest for conscious connection with the Infinite. When looking deeply into the levels and dimensions of a name, many revelations emerge. Abulafia's teachings include meditative Tzirufim or 'Permutations' of the letters of the names. This would often consist of repetitive chanting of the letters and sounds that make up a Divine Name in varying patterns while also visualizing those very letters as they dance, twist, and trade places with each other. This would in turn give birth to many new words and letter combinations — all hidden within the seed or root structure of the initial word, name, attribute, or quality.

The visualization practice we are going to do in a few moments involves the basic name of the Creator (ה־ו־ה־י), which we refer to as Hashem, meaning "the Name." The visualization of the patterns of the letters and their corresponding sound vibrations can actually allow us to experience something that leaves us with a tangible feeling of knowing, a sense that we have indeed touched or tasted the Divine.

STUDENT 1: I must say I am a bit skeptical.

TEACHER: That's good.

MEDITATION ON THE NAME OF THE INFINITE

TEACHER: The code of Jewish law (Shulchan Aruch) begins with the verse from Psalms, "I have placed Hashem before me at all times." This teaching can be understood on two ascending levels. The simple interpretation translates as being conscious that we are always within our Creator's presence. This awareness ensures that we eat, sleep, work, and communicate with others like a mentsch — with, sensitivity, mindfulness, and focused intention.

Going a bit deeper, we can engage the letters themselves that comprise the name and are interpreted to mean: I visualize the Hebrew letters that comprise the Name Hashem (י–ה–ו–ה), and I place them in front of my eyes at all times. I visualize them. I meditate on their forms and vibrations and numbers and stories. Not only do I acknowledge being in the Creator's Presence (first level of understanding), but on a more pro-active and co-creative level, I can actually participate in my perception of G-d's Presence. This is not to imply that G-d needs my participation to be Present, but that I can play a role in whether or not G-d is perceived.

A disciple once asked the Kotzker Rebbe, "where is G-d to be found in the world?" To which the Kotzker Rebbe replied, "wherever you let G-d in."

Through visualizing and meditating on the name of Hashem at all times, one comes to see the Divine within everything and everyone. The Ultimate Unity of all Creation gradually begins to reveal itself as one comes to see reality through a Divine lens, observing through the eyes of the Creator, so to speak.

MEDITATION: IN THE DIVINE IMAGE

Many Kabbalists have pointed out that when you arrange the four letters of G-d's un-pronounceable name vertically, instead of horizontally, they form the shape of a human being.

The (י) is the head. The first (ה) is the arms and shoulders. The (ו) is the spine and torso. The second (ה) is the hips and legs.

Gaze for a few moments at the letters of the Name. Become familiar with these shapes.

ה-ו-ה-י

Now close your eyes.
Envision yourself walking into an empty room of total white space.
Picture yourself holding a lit candle.

Using the flame from the candle, draw the letter Yud (י) on the white wall.
Observe the Yud as white fire against the white wall. Stay with this image for a few moments.

Again using the flame from your candle, draw the letter Hei (ה) to the left of the Yud.
Observe the Hei as white fire against the white wall. Focus on the Hei for a few moments.

Again using the flame, draw the letter Vav (ו) to the left of the Hei.
Observe the Vav as white fire against the white wall. Concentrate on the Vav for a few moments.

Using the flame, draw the final letter Hei (ה) to the left of the Vav.

Observe the Hei as white fire against the wall. Stay with the Hei for a few moments.

Now envision all four letters together, י-ה-ו-ה
Allow all four letters to hover before you simultaneously.
Renew the letters whenever they begin to fade. Continue to
inscribe them onto your inner screen...

Now bring the letters very close to your eyes, so that you're
seeing through them.

Opening your eyes, maintain the letters before you, like
transparent lenses.
See through the letters as you observe the world around you.

See through Hashem's Name, seeing the goodness, the divine aspect within all. Observe Creation as the Creator sees
it, and declare that, "it is very good"*(Genesis, 1:31)*.

(moment of silence)

TEACHER: How was that? What do you see? Does the world
look or feel different?

STUDENT 2: I can't stop seeing the name of G-d superim-
posed over every thing and person I look at. It's really powerful. What a great way to train ourselves to remember that
each and every person is created in the Divine Image. I think
the world would be a better place if everyone could see people in this way.

STUDENT 1: I agree. And besides seeing everyone else in this
elevated way, I feel like it's equally important for me to remember that I too am also created in this Divine image.

Sometimes it's easier for me to see the Divine in others than to see it in myself. I feel like seeing myself through the letters of G-d's name was healing and cleansing for me. It was like I could just let go and appreciate the miracle of me. For a split second I really felt whole and holy.

SELF- KNOWLEDGE

"FROM MY FLESH I SEE THE DIVINE" *(Job, 19:26)*.
"THE WORLD IS PLACED IN THE HEART" *(Ecclesiastics, 3:11)*.

TEACHER: Now I want to explore another avenue to approach an intimate and experiential knowledge of the Divine. In truth, the knowledge of self is instructive, and even essential, to obtaining any knowledge of G-d.

When meditating with expanded awareness on the intricate and wonderful workings of one's physical body, for example, one may take notice of, say, their elaborate digestive system, a sense of wonder and radical amazement is likely to take hold. The fine details of the work of art that is our body reveal the majestic artistry of the Artist. Simply by taking notice of what is most tangibly and immediately present we may come to "see God." From the embodied and physical we can move to the more subtle mental and emotional processes within our whole being. The complex and mysterious unfolding of our psyche reveals, albeit in a small measure, the complexity and infinite power of our Creator.

We are created in the image of the Creator. By delving deeply into our own selves, we may glimpse the depths of creation and ultimately the Infinite Creator.

Imagine gazing at a self-portrait painted by the world's master artist. It is not only an objective physical resemblance, but the inner world of the artist shines through the image. As we contemplate such a work of art, we are often able to sense something of the inner reality of the artist. If we are open and receptive, we can even be transported to a similar state of consciousness that the artist was in while the particular work was created.

We are fashioned in the image of the Creator and, as we are the masterpiece of the Infinite Artist, a Divine inner reality vibrates within us.

The Zohar teaches that, "The below is a reflection of the above." Each aspect of creation is a mirror reflecting its Creator. Although there may be screens such as our ego or previous conditioning that obscure our vision, peeling away the layers and piercing the veils reveals the Divine Essence within all existence.

Deeper still, creation is rooted in a holographic unified reality so that every apparently distinct part contains the whole. Each aspect of creation is thus a holographic image of the entire creation and of the Creator. Remember, *Adam Olam Katan, Olam Adam Gadol*, "Every Person is a small World, and the World is a large Person" (*Kuzari*). While this is true within all dimensions of creation, within the realm of the human being who was created in the "image of the Creator", this dynamic is even more pronounced.

"And the world is placed in the heart." The whole world, everything external to the self, is reflected within one's inner self. "Let us create man," declares the Creator to creation *(Genesis, 1:26)*. The 'us' is plural, indicating all of creation. As such, we contain traces of all aspects of creation: angel and animal, heaven and earth, fire and water, mineral and plant. We contain and reflect everything. Because of this, every action, word, or even thought we have effects the entire world.

MEDITATION ON THE IMPACT OF OUR ACTIONS

TEACHER: Think about this for a moment:

When you do a good deed, such as giving assistance to a needy person, meditate on the teaching that, "The below is a reflection of the above." Realize that Divinity and humanity are mirrors of each other. Become aware that the world above is mirroring your good deed, both individually and collectively. Feel how the act of giving changes and strengthens you, opening you up to receive.

Reflect on the interconnectedness and the 'us' of the world that you contain. Reflect on how your individual actions, your positive thoughts and words, are subtly but effectively impacting the very fabric of the entire world.

INTIMATE KNOWING

STUDENT 1: I do have to admit, I can't help but think, even with these powerful tools, how difficult it must be to get past the glimpse stage and enter into a more lasting and intimate knowing or state of being.

TEACHER: All of the above practices can bring us into relationship with the Creator. They are real and valid within their contexts and they bring us profound blessings. However, each one also implies some provisional split between the finite and the Infinite.

Divine Providence implies that there is a supreme intelligence separate from the world that it permeates. No matter how rarified and great it may be, spiritual love implies an 'I' who is loving a Divine 'Other'. The way we speak about the Divine itself implies dualism. The Sefirot remain attributes, distinct from the One to whom they are attributed. Regarding names, we are still stuck in the dualism of trees and branches. And the image evokes the Artist's spirit, but is not the ultimate totality of the Artist.

STUDENT 3: Is it true that real knowing means merging with the other? Doesn't the Torah use the Hebrew word for knowledge to refer to marital relations?

TEACHER: Yes it does imply a sort of union or intimacy that is necessary to actually attain a true knowledge of someone or something. But for now we can just remember that to truly know is to unify with that which is known.

Through these meditations, we can move toward the Infinite, yet no matter how close we come, there still is a sense of separation. Our awareness of the practice will always act as a boundary, separating the one who experiences from the experience itself.

HOLY ATHEISM

STUDENT 1: This makes me aware that we may think we know G-d, but we really don't. The separate and static image of the Creator that most of us believe in is not really G-d, it is just our limited idea of what the Creator should look or act like. Which means that I might be better off not believing in the G-d that I learned about as a child.

TEACHER: That's correct. Some people still have the old 'white-bearded man in the sky' idea of G-d somewhere in the back in their minds. In order to evolve our level of knowledge and expand our perception, we have to let go of our antiquated answers to eternal questions. The Sunday school answers may satisfy the questions of a small child, but as adults, we seek a different level of understanding or else we get stuck.

Rebbe Levi Yitzchak of Berditchev, the famed Chassidic Rebbe, told a self-proclaimed atheist, "The G-d you don't believe in, I also don't believe in!" This means that on a certain level there may be a grain of truth to atheism; a hidden spark, so to speak.

The hidden spark of atheism illuminates the fact that the fixed, rigid, over-simplified, and small-minded deity that most people subscribe to as G-d is, simply put, not anywhere near the ultimately unfathomable infinite mystery that is the One and only G-d.

On a deeper level, atheists themselves may even be mistaking the ultimate depth of their own critique.

STUDENT 1: How so?

TEACHER: Think about it. If the thought process stops at a brute refutation of an infantile conception of the Infinite, then it comes to bear that their own perspective is equally as underdeveloped, immature, and reactionary — more of a philosophical tantrum than a real attempt at engaging the multi-dimensionality of human experience in relation to both nature and the unseen. It is only when atheism is a beginning rather than an end in itself that it may actually serve to strengthen and evolve one's psycho-spiritual growth, refinement, and evolution.

STUDENT 3: Amazing: Atheism as a necessary stage of

healthy spiritual development. I never thought I'd hear this!

TEACHER: Well, there's more. R. Gikatalia expressed in his book, *The Gates of Light*, that no matter how exalted are our concepts of the Creator, this is not who G-d really is. It is as if we have written someone's name on a piece of paper. This may remind us of the person, but it does not capture the essence or totality of who or what that person really is.

This form of knowing is called Awareness of Existence, which still implies some sense of separation. It is not a full knowing, which is called Knowing the Essence. And in the spirit of the Biblical use of the word 'to know', which indicates a form of of union and intimacy, this alludes to a merging or coming together. This is when knowing transforms into being.

The brain, as an inherently binary and reifying machine, attempts to 'thing' everything, including Infinity. Logically, one thing is always separate from another thing. This takes us back to square one: Attempting to encounter an Infinite reality that to us, seems to exclude finitude.

The Creator is not a thing for the brain to grasp — not even an Infinite, abstract, or spiritual thing such as the Source of Creation.

STUDENT 1: Are you saying that there is really no such thing as the Creator?

TEACHER: There is G-d and G-d is all there is, and yet G-d should not be confused with the names and words we use to relate to or describe G-d.

Consider this a semantic yellow light: Slow down, remember that the word is not that which it describes, the map is not the territory. Don't go speeding through these crucial intersections taking language for granted. We are linguistically pointing at the menu. Don't confuse the menu for the meal.

Still, R. Abulafia and his student, R. Gikatalia, were not merely frustrated philosophers. They did attain a knowledge of the Creator.

STUDENT 3: If the Creator is not a thing, what did they come to know, and how?

KNOWLEDGE OF THE HEART

TEACHER: That's an essential question. Let's try to make some sense of it. I want to start with a quote from the Zohar, "There is no thought that can grasp You, but You can be grasped by the arousal of the heart".

This heart metaphor points to a kind of non-brain — a non-intellectual activity or deeper wisdom referred to as the Arousal of the Heart. The heart of who we are is a unified wholeness that transcends compartmentalization, duality, and thing-ing.

Intellectualism creates self-consciousness and a leaning towards objective observation from the outside. In effect, an intellectual understanding of the Divine ensures that there is always a built-in separation. If a person observes everything from the outside, he will forever remain outside the Everything.

When a person thinks about G-d and proclaims, "I love You," or "I thank You", this implies that there is a separate I and a separate You. There is the finite self, encountering the Infinite You. While this relationship suggests duality, a separate I and a separate You, it also implies a third element: the context in which the finite I is elevating towards the Infinite You.

STUDENT I: So if the I is Yesh consciousness, and the You is Ayin consciousness, then is this context thing you are talking about representative of Yesh Amiti?

THE ESSENCE OF THE DIVINE

TEACHER: Exactly. The Essence of the Divine is referred to as *Etzem* or *Atzmut*, the Ultimate I, which is within the finite but also beyond the Infinite. While Etzem transcends these categories and concepts, it also paradoxically includes them. Unlike the *Ein Sof*, or Infinite, the Essence is not exclusive, for there is nothing outside of Essence to exclude or transcend. So the Essence can be thought of as both sides of a coin, as well as the circumference that connects and includes them both together, as One.

The Essence is no-thing and every-thing, and yet it is neither nothingness nor everything-ness. It cannot be thought, yet it includes all thoughts. It is all form and yet remains utterly formless. For this reason, Essence, or the Ultimate I, *Ani*, cannot be spoken about or even experienced consciously. Self-consciousness distances the mind and self from the experience itself.

This is the paradox of life — fullness and emptiness, desire and complacency, transcendence and immanence. In the finite world, the concept of time exists and we sense a separation of past, present, and future. From an infinite perspective, however, there is no difference between what was, what is, and what will be because there is no time.

Essence includes both the finite perspective of real time, and the Infinite perspective of no time. There is only now, but a now that includes all of the past and all of the future. This is referred to as the Eternal Present. The Eternal Present is the moment that transcends, but also encompasses, all dimensions of time: past, present and future: everything is present right now.

All this brings us back to our original question: What is the meaning of *Ein Od Mi-l'vado*, "There is nothing else besides Hashem?" We are not merely talking about theological and philosophical monotheism, meaning that there are no other independent forces in the universe. We are speaking about absolute monotheism, meaning that there is nothing else period. Yet, this does not imply pantheism, which is where everything is equated with the Divine. The world of things is an expression of the Ultimate I of G-d, but it is not the totality of G-d. In the words of the ancient sages, "G-d is the place of the universe, but the universe is not the place of G-d." The universe is an expression of the Creator, but is not to be confused with the Creator.

The first of the Ten Commandments begins, *Anochi Hashem Elokecha*, "I am Hashem your G-d." *Anochi*, I, is Essence. *Hashem* is the Infinite. And *Elokecha* is Elokim, the aspect of Divinity that touches the finite world. Essence is the third element, the context. This is the coin itself, wherein both sides are constructed and contained, embracing and resolving the existential tension between the plural Elokim and the Infinite Hashem of Oneness — between manifest reality and un-manifest reality, between matter and spirit, between linear, or even cyclical, time and space and timelessness and spacelessness.

STUDENT 1: Does this Ultimate I have a Name, besides I?

TEACHER: Of course not. Think about it, the moment you name something it means that you are separate from it, and the Ultimate I includes everything, including you. As mentioned, it cannot even be spoken about, for by speaking about it you are (to your mind) separate from that which you are speaking about, and ultimately there is no such separation.

Accordingly, unlike Elokim and the Tetragramaton, which may only be written and pronounced in prayer and study, the word Etzem or Atzmut is not a sacred word, and therefore can be pronounced and written without reservations. Etzem is reality itself, including your reading and pronouncing this word right now.

STUDENT 2: So, what about love? Before there was talk about the awesome awareness of arousing love and feeling loved by the Creator, and now it seems that we are back to a place that is transcendent of feelings. Are feelings of love and being loved merely stages of underdeveloped spiritual awareness? Does the deepest way of living negate all feelings? Does it imply an abandonment of all the fullness and flavor of life?

TEACHER: Not at all. On the contrary, Atzmut transcends and includes all feelings and thoughts. Atzmut includes the total fullness of *Yesh*, Something, and the radical emptiness of *Ayin*, Nothing. This includes the place of poetry and music and the place of stillness and silence. We too need to live in both places, as it were, simultaneously. As much as we are one — and we are — we also function from a place where we experience duality and multiplicity. They are both true. Yet when our relationship with Divinity, our love and awe, flows from an Atzmut Awareness, the relationship is spontaneous, effortless, stress free, and natural.

LIVING ESSENCE

STUDENT 3: So how can we meditate on or reach Essence? Is there a practice that can lead us to Essence?

TEACHER: There are no separate practices or meditations on Essence, because Essence is not a separate phenomenon on which we can meditate. In this sense we cannot become aware of Essence. We can only be Essence. What we can do is to take any meditative practice and perform it within the context of 'being that which we are doing'.

Ultimately, Essence in its purest form is found in simple actions, unencumbered by motivation or emotion. Essence just is. We cannot awaken to Essence by contemplating or meditating on Essence's non-formulation, since contemplating and meditating themselves are nothing more than another formulation.

As Essence embraces and includes infinity and finitude, our life-path as well can balance and include both transcendence and immanence, both reaching higher and staying grounded. Without the balance, either extreme is not wholesome. Both the glutton and the ascetic are obsessed with food. They are both trying to achieve something. Spiritual materialism involves attempting to become one with a separate and exclusive Infinity. We imagine that we are substantially cut off, so our search becomes serious and strained. The imagined threat of failure causes us to impose joyless strictures on ourselves and on others. Or we may seek to transcend the world altogether and find escape in a separate realm of imagined bliss.

STUDENT 2: Right. This is what worries me. People end up just spinning out and don't actually participate in the transformation and healing of the world.

TEACHER: This is a valid concern. When we live life with Etzem Consciousness we are spiritually fulfilled. We are then able to come from a place of wholeness, without a sense of guilt, worthlessness, or lack. In Etzem Consciousness our actions are not motivated by superstition or heavy-handed discipline, nor escapism or over-compensation. Therefore we can strive and serve with a measure of lightness and celebration. We may then spontaneously treat every person we encounter, every leaf on every tree, with unconditional respect and sensitivity. Life is a Divine celebration at every moment and we are living with this awesome awareness.

May each of us merit to truly know that nothing is outside, or separate from, The Essence.

CONVERSATION II:

CREATION

CONVERSATION II:
CREATION

The table is full of faces, eyes closed, corners of lips turned slightly upward in a circle of curious smiles. The gathering begins with a slow and deep, meditative melody. The hauntingly beautiful song rises and falls like waves on a dark ocean. It is as if the whole world is slowing down and settling into a deep calm. Slowly, the voices subside like rushing waters at low tide. There is a comfortable silence, until a soft voice emerges from the quiet.

TEACHER: The subject tonight is the nature of the world we live in. As we have done previously on our journey towards knowing the Divine, we will allow questions to surface organically and reveal themselves in order that we may receive the answers and inspirations contained within them. By the very act of asking, we are opening ourselves up to receive. So let's begin with some questions.

STUDENT 1: What is the world and where does it come from?

STUDENT 2: If there is only Unity, how can there be any sense of duality, of the separation of time and space? How can a world defined by duality even exist?

STUDENT 3: Yes, and why don't we always perceive the Unity within in this world? Also, what would be the source of separation and alienation in this world?

THE PROBLEM:
UNITY AND DIVERSITY

TEACHER: Let's start with: Can Unity give birth to duality?

STUDENT 1: I don't think so. It would no longer be a perfect unity if some other thing came out of it.

STUDENT 3: I agree. Unity has no inside or outside because if there were such a split, there would be two, not one.

TEACHER: True, it is impossible for Ultimate Unity to change or diminish in any way. But then it would also be impossible for any real duality, any creation, to exist at all. So the mystery is not only how the world is, but simply, that it is at all.

STUDENT 2: I am still a bit confused. If indeed Creation is unreal, being a mere realm of perceived multiplicity, when in fact everything is One in perfect Unity — so what then is our purpose of living in this physical world?

TEACHER: This is the ultimate question. The early Kabbalists acknowledged the reality of what appears to be duality. They saw that everything that comes into being is by definition the effect of a cause. If we sense that phenomena exist, if we are perfectly honest, we must admit that these phenomena do indeed exist and have a cause or source. In other words: If we see a world, there is a world.

STUDENT 1: A world that comes from where? How does this Unity give birth to a world?

SOLUTION I:
THE CHAIN OF CAUSALITY

TEACHER: For the moment, let's stay with the provisional truth of cause-and-effect duality. Probing the dual structure of cause and effect does not resolve, or even adequately illustrate, the issue of ultimate non-dual reality, but it is a useful lens for those of us who perceive that there is separation and duality. We have to admit to ourselves that often we live as though the world we live in is separate from its Source, would you agree?

STUDENT 2: Yes. I would even take it a step further and argue that we *must* live as if we were separate from the Source in order to get anything done in this world.

TEACHER: There's nothing wrong with that. But we may want to look into the root of this perception. There appears to be a world or effect, and a Creator or Cause. Cause and effect, or *Ila v'Alul*, are interdependent and relative to each other. There cannot be an effect without a cause. If there is separation between Creator and Creation, how does this separation occur? How can Unity transmit into multiplicity?

STUDENT 3: There's an evolution happening, like a diversification, but somehow it doesn't change the deeper unity.

TEACHER: Good answer. The bridge between the One and the many can be understood as a single point. Not a point with spatial existence, but a point in the abstract, mathematical sense. If a second point somehow joined this point it would be as if there was a line between them. The appearance of this linear reality creates a first dimension. The line, if then joined by a third point outside the trajectory of the line, would form a triangular plane or surface area — a second-dimension. Joined by a fourth point, volume appears, a third dimension. The continuing evolution of this increasing complexity represents the creative process of multi-dimensionality. This is the way R. Shlomo Ibn Gabriel (11th century), the Zohar, and Nachmonides (13th century) explained the unfolding process of creation.

STUDENT 2: That works for me.

STUDENT 1: I'm not following. How can it be a perfect unified reality if something comes from within it and manifests outside of it?

TEACHER: This first understanding, based as it is on a theory of causality and evolutionary process, appears initially to be dualistic. If we interpret it literally we would have to reject this idea as it places a limit on the Creator's Unity. So let us try to come to terms with the full paradox. Let's discuss this as explored by R. Yitzchak Luria, the *Ari*, who went beyond the earlier view of multi-dimensional creation.

SOLUTION II: TZIMTZUM

TEACHER: Instead of defining the process of creation as a gradual and quantitative evolution, we can understand creation in terms of a qualitative evolution, or quantum leap, from Unity to multiplicity. The *Ari* revealed, by unpacking ancient teachings that allude to this idea, that initially there was a primordial contraction within the Creator's Unity. He called this Cosmic Contraction, *Tzimtzum.* The Tzimtzum then created a *Chalal*, an empty space, where a separate universe could exist. This Divine Self-restraint, or nullification, allows the possibility for finitude to exist within the context of Infinity.

Every form of birth emerges from a contraction. On a macrocosmic level, the birth of the entire cosmos, and on a microcosmic level, the birth of a child, all occur with a corresponding Tzimtzum, and with it the pangs of birth. Even in our day-to-day life, every creative act and every new moment begins with a withdrawal in order to assert.

Now, on a cosmic level, once there is a place for a finite world to exist, the infinite light can re-enter the vacated space in a focused, controlled, hidden, or condensed manner. Then the light passes through many filters, in which the light becomes more and more condensed, almost solidified.

STUDENT 3: Would these filters be like the Sefirot?

TEACHER: Yes. Exactly. This metamorphosis is the process in which everything — human beings, animals, plants, even insentient matter — is created. The descent from undifferentiated pure spirit, down to unconscious matter is known as the *Kav*, the Pipe or Channel, through which all levels of creation travel on their path to manifestation.

This can be visualized as a glass blower's tube through which the breath of the Creator travels into the vessel of Creation, giving it a particular form as well as the animating breath of life. One can also imagine the Kav as a ladder through which the Creator's energy and intention is constantly descending and ascending up and down the chain of being. And finally, the Kav can be thought of as that initial bridge we spoke of, a quantum bridge so to speak, across which the Infinite travels into form and finitude.

STUDENT 3: This is really descriptive. I feel like I can relate to this in my own creative process. When I get inspired I often feel like there is something coming down a chute from above. This must be the Kav.

TEACHER: It's true. There is a connection and holographic resonance between the cosmic creative process and the creative process as it occurs within our own consciousness. Remember this is what the Torah is referring to when it says that humans are created *B'tzelem Elokim*, "in the image of the creative aspect of G-d".

But let's get back to this process. From the perspective of the Chalal, our world is separate and autonomous. There appears to be no other reality and there are convincing arguments for atheism. Our conscious awareness of self is simply a random by-product of a highly complex nervous system. However, from the perspective of the Kav, our world of linear time and defined space is only one of many worlds linked together as a chain of being originating in the Divine Source. This awareness of being within the Kav lifts us up, enabling and motivating us to reach out and connect with the Source of all Light and Life.

Consciousness is the primary reality, while matter is simply a more solidified and densely structured form of energy. In effect, there is not solid matter as we think of it. Everything is alive and vibrating at various frequencies, from the subtle and spiritual to the dense and material. In the words of classic Kabbalah: "From the condensation of Lights, the vessels (which appear as separate and defined entities) were brought into being."

SOLUTION III: TZIMTZUM LO K'PSHUTO

STUDENT 2: Is this notion of Tzimtzum really fundamentally different than gradual evolution? Have we really reached a solution to the quandary of inseparable Unity giving birth to multiplicity? On the one hand there is the *Ohr Ein Sof*, the Infinite Unified Light, and yet what we most often experience is a reality of *Sof*, of End, of finitude, of definition, of time and space.

TEACHER: The idea of Tzimtzum is certainly a more profound understanding, but no, it is not the ultimate solution to the question of duality, at least not the way we understand Tzimtzum at this point.

STUDENT 1: If the Tzimtzum teaching is literally true and the Infinite One has contracted and limited itself, then is it no longer considered Infinite? Conversely, if it is not literally true then there should not be a limited world? Which one is it?

TEACHER: To intensify this inquiry, I'll add that many mystical masters refer to our universe as *Alma d'Shikra*, a World of Deception.

STUDENT 3: Perhaps they're saying that our world — the Tzimtzum world — is not real after all? It appears to me, that if the Tzimtzum is real then the world is real, and if the Tzimtzum is not real, not literal, then the world is not real and is a mere illusion?

TEACHER: This is a paradox that depends on perspective. There are two basic perspectives; from the eyes of the Infinite One, there is no limitation, no Tzimtzum, there is only Infinity. Even absence is a type of presence. But we, who perceive ourselves as separate beings, endow Tzimtzum with a sense of tangible reality, as a real concealment. From the eyes of the finite, there is a Tzimtzum. Being vested in a three dimensional universe, we think in a spatial, temporal framework. We think in terms of linear causality: time, and relational space. And so from this perspective, endowing Tzimtzum with a sense of reality is indeed accurate. Anything that we can detect with our senses is a Something, a *Yesh*. It is real for us, and we must deal with it accordingly. So the Tzimtzum is real to us, and so is our world.

STUDENT 2: If I stood in the middle of traffic and proclaimed that there is no limited world and that the oncoming car is not real, I would be deceiving myself. Honesty includes getting out of the middle of the street.

STUDENT 3: But fear and stress are not necessary in getting out of the street. That would also be a deception.

TEACHER: If we objectively sense a car, there is objectively a car there. Likewise, whatever is beyond our senses is as nothing, *Ayin* — it doesn't exist for us. Now, if we were to shift to a more panoramic perspective, we would see that there are real things, or realities, that hadn't previously existed for us until we perceived them. From an Infinite level of consciousness we would see that what we called nothing, is really everything in potential, and what we called something, was really nothing in actuality.

STUDENT 1: So the world of deception refers to lower levels of consciousness and limited perspective?

TEACHER: Yes, because this world is, from our limited perspective at least, a Divine game of hide-and-seek. The so-called deception in this game is that in our own consciousness, the Everything is somehow successfully hiding behind something, which is really nothing.

NO SEPARATION

STUDENT 2: It still seems that we are saying that the world is an illusion that we have created through our limited senses; that the oncoming car is only real if we are perceiving it on a lower level. This does not sound right. Again, if the world is an illusion, why should we bother with improving or protecting life in this world? And what use to us is an Infinite Everything that doesn't even recognize us 'nothings'?

TEACHER: Ah. This is where Torah stops us in our tracks with its opening words: "In the beginning when the Creator created the heavens and the earth" *(Genesis, 1:1)*. This is a clear affirmation of the authenticity of our physical 3-dimensional universe. The world is not a figment of our imagination, but is in fact a creation of the Creator. And as such, being a manifestation of The Real, The Creator, it must also be real.

Let's look deeper. This *Pasuk,* or sentence, from the beginning of the Torah also points out that Hashem created both "the Heavens and the Earth". This means that there is potentially much more going on then we may perceive from the earth plane. The Heavens implies a realm that is beyond, or more subtle, than the Earth. So the world of illusion may only be an illusion if seen from a limited perspective. The physical world in itself is not the illusion; it is our perception of it as the only realm of reality that is the illusion.

As you brought up earlier, the car really is there and it will run you over, but that is not all. There is much more beyond our immediate senses and normal perceptive faculties. There may in fact be an angel standing in between you and that car for instance.

STUDENT 2: I wouldn't count on it.

STUDENT 3: But there might be.

STUDENT 1: It's like Schrodinger's Cat. You don't now unless you look. You have to open the door.

STUDENT 2: But what is the door?

STUDENT 3: The door is your perception. Open your mind.

TEACHER: Ok, Ok. We could all do well to open our minds, but let's not forget to open our hearts while we're at it.

Now where were we? Oh right. From a more wide-angle lens, the world does not necessarily exist the way we may have perceived it from a narrower perspective — that is, as separate and autonomous. If we hold onto the paradox between the two verses: "There is nothing else but the Creator," and "...the Creator created", we must conclude that the world itself is a finite expression of the Infinite One and that it remains eternally enclosed and embraced within, as well as permeated and filled by, the Infinite.

The Tzimtzum is not literal, not real, from the perspective of the "eyes of the Infinite One", and yet, from that very same perspective, the world is real, and these two statements are both true. There is no separate world. But at the same time the world is real, a finite expression of *Atzmut*.

STUDENT 3: So both the oncoming car and I are not separate from the Creator, and yet there's a certain reality to the dream, so I get out of the street?

TEACHER: Absolutely. Here's another way of saying it. "In the beginning", in Hebrew, is *B'reishit*. The mystics sometimes experiment with the sequences of Hebrew letters within a given word in order to unleash hidden potentials of meaning. The consonants B, R, Y, SH, T can be rearranged to spell BaRaTa YeSH. This translates as, "You have created a *Yesh*, a something, a seemingly separate existence."

There is a real world, a something, but we are the ones who have created, or bought into it, the illusory separateness of that world.

STUDENT 1: So why should G-d run from or hide from G-d? Or, perhaps one should worship the car instead?

TEACHER: There is a Chassidic aphorism: "All is the Creator and the Creator is all." This means that all of creation is included within the Unity of the Creator. This does not mean that every individual creation is itself the Creator. We are all part of G-d, but we are not G-d. G-d is the Infinite One and is not to be found in totality within any one finite part. But if even one finite part were missing, it would not be the Infinite G-d, as it were. This also means that mathematically speaking, G-d is greater than the sum of G-d's parts.

Alternatively, this Chassidic aphorism is saying something even more mathematically simple: 'All is the Creator and the Creator is All'. This means that only when you perceive all of creation, together as one, can creation be likened to a reflection of the Creator. The Creator is not the same thing as the creation. That again would be pantheism.

This is similar to the ancient teaching that, "G-d is the place of the world, but the world is not the place of G-d". The world exists within, and is an expression of, the Divine, but is not the Divine itself. The Creator pervades the world but also completely transcends it. The world is contained within G-d but does not, by definition, transcend G-d.

STUDENT 2: So is the world real or not?

TEACHER: Yes it is real. But no, it is not an autonomous creation separate from the One.

STUDENT 1: Since perception is real, my question is: How should we relate to the natural sciences, to our empirical understanding of the universe?

TEACHER: Well, as the Kabbalists say: the *Sod* is in the *Peshat*, the Secret is in the Simple. Or the *Niglah* is the *Nistar*, the Revealed is the Concealed. The deepest vision and understanding of life does not exclude the more surface perspectives. So, for that matter, our scientific materialist understanding is not rendered obsolete in the face of the deeper spiritual understanding.

STUDENT 2: The meta-physical does not eclipse the physical?

TEACHER: On the contrary, when the physical and meta-physical can harmonize their particular perspectives, there can be a fundamentally fuller appreciation for the immeasurable immensity of life.

What is perhaps needed is the transparency of the surface — the externally oriented bodies of knowledge. This goes beyond remembering the moon to which the finger points and goes a step further, to remember the sun that shines the light which the moon reflects, and then even further to remember the Source of the sun's light.

STUDENT 3: Spirit smiles at us beneath the surface of science.

TEACHER: Exactly. In fact, many of the great Kabbalists of old were trained physicians, or astronomers. Their materialist knowledge was enhanced and made transparent by their visionary thinking and deeper understanding of the non-quantifiable aspects of the universe.

TRUE SELF

STUDENT 1: Aren't we just creating a sense of separateness when we refer to the Creator as a You, as in "Blessed are You?"

TEACHER: This physical universe does not automatically appear to be connected to the Creator. The *Chalal,* or Empty space, creates the appearance that there is nothing beyond this world. Only in this Tzimtzum realm can the thought even occur that there is no Divine Source, or that the world creates itself on accident. This self-referential tendency is the root of all self-centeredness. So in this realm, Divine causality is a more accurate understanding of reality. Again, it is not the ultimate solution to the problem of duality, but it helps us relate to that which is utterly beyond us when we relate to a Divine 'You'.

Furthermore, without obscuration, the unity of creation and Creator is clear. But in Chalal consciousness, developing a connection and relationship through prayer and praise brings light to the darkness — the darkness of thinking and acting as if we are not all connected. Referring to the Creator as a You is an initial first step to move out of the Chalal and to begin traveling back up the Kav to reconnect our consciousness to that of the Creator, at which point the You becomes the I of Ani- the ultimate I AM. Not the personal 'i', although that too is contained within the Ultimate I of Hashem.

This first step of acknowledging the existence of the Creator as You, is our necessary Tzimtzum, in which we are able to step back and make room for an other to exist. It is a sensitive statement to say that, it is not really all about me all the time. By mirroring the cosmic creative process, we are able to make space in order to connect to and develop a relationship with the Divine. If we are always full of ourselves, our little i, then there is no room for anyone or anything else in our heart, mind, or life. Acknowledging and addressing Hashem as You is the first baby step out of a completely small-self-centered universe.

Also, don't forget that we are relating to G-d not as an It, but rather as a You. This itself is a linguistic quantum leap from understanding G-d as an Infinitely impersonal Energy to relating to G-d as an Infinitely personal Presence — a Parent and Protector. True, the *Ohr Ein Sof* is the Infinite, Unified and creative Source of all reality. Yet, radically and paradoxically, the utterly unknowable Infinite Unity is also close and intimate with the smallest individual details of every single one of our lives. And yes, it is possible to have a personal relationship with Hashem. The infinite and universal Creator is concerned and involved with the finite and unique creatures within creation. And as such, we acknowledge this relationship with Hashem, by addressing G-d as a subject, not as an object.

STUDENT 2: So making the world a better place has to do with thinking and acting according to the reality that we are in fact all inter-connected, and that there is no fundamental separation.

STUDENT 1: We have said several times that we are not yet approaching the ultimate solution to duality. We have only been talking about appearances. But how, in perfect Unity, can there even appear to be an illusion of separation? Is this something that can be talked about, or should I just drop my question?

TEACHER: I believe that we have genuinely attempted to wrestle with and explore these paradoxes, and have held onto the question for some time now. So yes, what would happen if we dropped the "duality question", at least for a moment, and continued exploring some other terrain?

STUDENT 3: I get the sense that there's something that encompasses both the Unity and the Multiplicity.

STUDENT I: Should we just imagine that there's no conflict between Unity and Duality?

TEACHER: Just be still...

(long silence...)

TEACHER: Just be still and know. Know that the Essence is the I, *Ani*, the true Self of Hashem. As you have sensed, the Essence is also called *HaMakom*, the Place, of both unity and apparent duality. The Absolute I is the context and essence of the limited human i, the ego, as well as the infinite Divine 'You'. As we have said before, this Divine Essence is what unifies the finite and the Infinite, the creation and the Creator.

A few moments ago we were talking about the self-referential quality of the world. The amazing thing is that this self-absorbed world is exactly where the Absolute Essence of the Creator is most easily expressed and experienced. Why? Because, simply put, the Essence itself is completely self-referential. Everything and every non-thing, both the cause and its effects, express only One Essence. Their self-hood is simply a metaphor for the Absolute Self. Only the Essence, whose existence is derived from itself alone can allow the appearance of a creation that appears to be separate, self-derived, and autonomous.

It is true that the mere act of speaking about or conceptualizing the Essence is pretending to define what cannot be defined. If we speak as if there are three realities, the Essence, Creator, and creation, we are back to provisional answers. We cannot know the Essence like we know an object. What we do know is that it is the Essence that expresses itself as both finite and infinite. It is its own expression. The Essence of the Artist is present within the work of art, and is in fact that which creates and connects them both.

Recognizing that we *are* It and that therefore we can't *see* It, this is the spontaneous natural-state meditation that is happening right now. This is meditation without a separate meditator. This speaking is perfect silence. This is the stillness of Essence speaking, hearing, thinking, meditating, being...

(long tangible silence)

STUDENT 3: There is a tremendous sense of ease in this. Since we are already It, and the world is already There, we seem to have an end-run around spiritual practice, and trying to save the world.

TEACHER: Yes and no. With this insight we still continue to practice and we continue to work to make the world a better place, but not from a frustrated and desperate place of limitation. On the contrary, because we know there is no separation, our compassion, our service, and our optimism know no bounds. Our work in bringing about inner and outer peace and redemption continues with the Essence Itself as the backdrop and foreground.

STUDENT 2: I am a bit confused. I understand that if I take reality as real and duality as true and the world as a Yesh, then my work has value and my desire to help change myself and the world around me is meaningful. To me, in this world-view, the application of ethics and *Mitzvot*, or spiritual-ritual activities, makes sense. Yet, it would seem that ethics and Mitzvot become obsolete from the perspective that there is no duality? Are we not, from this perspective, transcendent of duality, or beyond good and evil, maybe even beyond ethics all together?

TEACHER: Let me clarify this very important point. I am sure you recall that we spoke earlier of three perspectives or paradigms: *Yesh*, Existence, *Ayin*, No-thing-ness, and *Yesh Amiti*, True Existence. Let us flesh out these paradigms more clearly.

> 1) The first paradigm is one that is gained through our senses, the world of multiplicity. This is reality as *Yesh*.
> 2) The second paradigm is non-dual, where there is no longer an inside and outside, or object and subject, there is only a sense of *Ayin*, No-thing-ness.
> 3) The deepest paradigm is *Yesh Amiti*. This transcends and includes both paradigms. It says that: "Yes there is a real world, with time and space, and yet the world is not separate from the Unity of the Creator, but is in

fact included within the Infinite Unity".

In the first paradigm, the purpose of our Mitzvot or good deeds is to refine and elevate ourselves and the world around us. In the language of the *Midrash*, "The Mitzvot were given only for the purpose of refining the human being." From this perspective, we are separate from our Source, the world is separate, and what we seek is unity. Ethical behavior and the Mitzvot are the tools that we use to create the connection.

From the perspective of Ayin there is no longer the concept of Mitzvot. You are correct, from the perspective of nothingness and emptiness, all is nothing. Again, to use the words of the Talmudic sages, "The dead are free of Mitzvot" *(Nidda, 61b)*. In death, or in a condition where there is no longer a self-conscious and separate human being acting with free choice, the entire concept of doing, changing, growing, or refining is obsolete. In Ayin there is a transcendence of duality, of good and evil.

Yet, as the Kabbalistic and Chassidic teachers write, "Mitzvot are linked with Atzmut or Essence." Within the deepest truth, ethics and Mitzvot resurface. Not because it has to be this way, but rather simply because it is. The Highest is tied to the Lowest. "The end is wedged in the beginning."*(Sefer Yetzirah)*. Our existence is a (direct) manifestation of Ultimate Existence. When we do Mitzvot from this paradigm they are effortless, spontaneous, and without resistance. Here our actions allow us to recognize a truth that is already present all the time, which is that we are one with the Unity of the Creator, yet because we live in a real duality as well, our actions should help us notice, acknowledge, and reveal this truth.

HALACHA AND AGGADA

The Torah, both written and oral, is comprised of two main components: *Halacha* and *Aggada*. *Halacha*, which translates literally as the walking, is the body of legal opinions, debates, and rulings concerning all areas of life, including civil, marital, ritual, political, cultural, and economic. *Aggada* is the vast body of stories, legends and lore.

Halacha speaks more to the part of us where the Divine is transcendent. This means that our adherence to Halacha implies a connection to the Transcendent Being who blessed us with the burden of holiness by giving us Torah, which is comprised of Mitzvot, i.e. Divine commandments, rituals, and laws by which we are to order our human society and personal lives. The Mitzvot are seen as actions or channels of connection. It is through our performance of the Mitzvot, and the consequential ordering of our society and personal lives based on the Torah, that allows us to connect to the Transcendent in this world.

Aggada speaks more to the part of us where the Divine is immanent. This means that stories and the consciousness they help to create are rooted in our ability to see the hand of the Creator in everything we experience. This perspective is based more on the view that the Creator is always present, even in the mundane aspects and actions of our lives. Through our everyday lives, our trials and tribulations, our struggles, victories, defeats, and small miracles, we are able to sense the Presence of the Creator's Immanence. G-d is always here, we just have to open our eyes and hearts to notice.

The Torah is comprised of both of these elements. This is like the tension between Yesh and Ayin. Ultimately, the Torah teaches that both bodies of text are important, and only through the active engagement with both Halacha and Aggada does one enter into the Essence of a Torah life.

LIVING THE TEACHING

With this insight we can now return to our discussion of how to refine the world. Remember that the Essence contains and comprises the two seemingly contradictory creative processes we spoke about earlier:

1) The chain of evolution — gradual, linear cause and effect.
2) The Tzimtzum — the contraction and quantum leap of infinite to finite.

These viewpoints are both still valid, as they are also expressions of the Essence.

Nothing disappears in, or of, the Essence. The Essence is Eternal and Ever Present. Essence transcends all space and time and therefore is beyond, and within, all sensory stimulated dichotomous breakdowns of Unity and Inter-Connectedness.

Let's look back into the world-view of Tzimtzum and its implied path of spiritual practice in more depth. Just as there are different phases to the Ari's map of Creation, there are different phases to this map of consciousness.

As we said earlier, before Creation there was nothing but the Infinite light, the *Ohr Ein Sof*. There was no way, no space, no time for anything else to exist. In our lives, this is similar to when our awareness is closed up, our cup is full — we are literally full of ourselves. It is as if the Divine, or any other, doesn't exist in our world.

The Tzimtzum corresponds to our opening, our making space, so we can receive an influx of the Divine Presence. This is part of becoming nothing or Ayin. Just as the Infinite creates a vacated space, a nothing, in order to create a something; so too when we make ourselves as nothing in the presence of the Infinite Light we can create the space and potential for something new and better to enter into our lives and into the world. This is, on the surface, a bit paradoxical. The equation goes like this: Everything becomes nothing in order to create something.

BREAKING OF THE VESSELS

Now after the initial contraction the infinite light re-enters the vacated space. What we did not mention yet is that initially, this returning light caused a meltdown in the *Keilim*, or Vessels, that were created to channel and direct the Infinite Light within the Chalal. This is called the *Shevirat Ha'keilim*, the devastating Shattering of the Vessels. The vessels, also known as the *Sefirot*, could not withstand the force of the refocused infinite light. They were not balanced, integrated, or flexible enough to handle such a Light.

The weakness of the Sefirot was that they were isolated from each other. There was no exchange or interplay. For example, there was no balance between boundless love and kindness, *Chesed*, and the boundaries, discipline and restraint of *Gevura*. Each Sefira was only concerned with maximizing its own potential as if existing in a vacuum. There was no sense of all aspects being part of one structure, so there could be no autonomic self-balancing. It was as if your two arms were not in communication and they each had self-centered drives of their own.

STUDENT 3: Both arms would end up fighting each other over which one would pick up the cup and your mouth would have a hard time convincing either of them to raise it up and pour.

TEACHER: Exactly. In this state the light couldn't be contained and cosmic chaos ensued. Shards of light were trapped, so to speak, in the vessels and the vessels crashed down towards our world of materiality, while the main light returned to its Source. As the fragments of light fell, they broke into countless smaller sparks, which lodged themselves throughout our world. Gradually *Kelipot*, translated as Husks or Shells, formed around these sparks, concealing them.

STUDENT 3: This really resonates with me. I don't exactly know why, but I can really relate to what you're saying.

TEACHER: Well, we can see this dynamic in ourselves. For instance, when we have opened ourselves up to what is beyond us, sometimes it is overwhelming. Too much light too fast can cause our awareness to shatter or to shut down again, sometimes more closed off than it was before, due to the fear and trauma of the intensity of the influx. Intense spiritual experience can be helpful, but also harmful. Sometimes it is necessary to slow down, stabilize, and integrate. Sometimes less is more.

STUDENT 2: Like in homeopathy?

TEACHER: Yes. And if we allow ourselves to be a little more less, then we are able to see the psycho-spiritual function of entering into a state of *Ayin* in order to re-emerge back into a healthy and well-balanced state of *Yesh Amiti*.

We can achieve this by nullifying our finite selves in the face of the Infinite, as well as within the larger structure of the rest of creation. Remember, it is not all about you all the time. Often lessons need to be extrapolated from pure light in order to be put into practice.

Furthermore, because it is well known that peak experiencesmay often feel amazing and tend to be super 'Aha' moments of self-realization, there is a danger that they become ends in themselves, manifesting as just another roller coaster at the theme park of life. It takes time, effort, and support to bring down the light.

STUDENT 2: And often times, the take home lesson is about interacting with others: G-d, family, neighbors, nature, and the world at large.

STUDENT 1: So, in essence, the equation is this: Spiritual experience is a revelation of the Self to the self for the sake of the other, which is really the Self.

STUDENT 2: But if the light never re-circulates to the other, but only stays contained and hoarded within the small self, it becomes mere self-indulgence and ego-enslavement.

TEACHER: We need to come down from the mountain and take the time to do the hard, sometimes painful, work of putting the peak experiences into practice.

This is often a more sustainable and integrative spiritual approach. For most of us it would be psychologically impossible to sustain a perpetual peak experience. That is why they are called peaks. We need time for grounding in order to develop ways to stay connected to the highest heights not only when we are receiving the Light from the top of the peaks, but also when we are lost in the dark canyons, or meandering through the level fields of our everyday life.

STUDENT 3: This realization is liberating and strengthening. It allows me to see clearly that I am part of a bigger picture, that it is up to me to receive that Light which I am created to receive, and how important it is to keep that Light moving and circulating to the other aspects of creation and consciousness which will themselves receive, transform, and re-circulate the Light.

STUDENT 2: The take home realization from this 'Shattering of the Vessels' seems to be that we don't have to do it all by ourselves — it's not all up to us. We are responsible for what we can do and we also have a responsibility to share the load with the rest of creation. We need to communicate and share responsibility or else we will shatter and destroy this world.

TEACHER: Put another way: The first run of the Sefirot shattered precisely because they were too into themselves as individual vessels. They needed more *Ayin*, more nothing. It is taught that they did not function in balance or a sense of cooperation, but only to satisfy their own innate capacity and drive. This dynamic was precisely what caused the breakdown and shattering of the vessels. For the Tree of Life to function properly all *Shefa*, Divine Influx, has to move unimpeded through all levels of the cosmic structure of creation and consciousness. If any one elemental aspect is not in balance and clear communication with the whole or with any of its particular parts, there results a breakdown, a build-up, a blockage, and then explosion — shattering. Each vessel must go through its own process of clearing itself sufficiently to receive the *Ohr Ein Sof*. It is their, and our, true purpose and function to receive the Shefa from the Source and circulate it to the rest of creation.

STUDENT 2: Now this sounds like an idea I can relate to. We're talking about a radical redistribution of wealth, but the resource is energy and awareness. We can't hoard it. We have to share it and support each other or else the whole structure suffers.

ELEVATING THE FALLEN SPARKS

TEACHER: Precisely. The mission entrusted to each of us is to reveal the fallen sparks of Divinity within every aspect of Creation by relating to them in ways that acknowledge their Source and Sustainer. The instinct of *Tikkun*, or Fixing, is universal and innate. Deep down we all desire to make things better. Even when we fix a gadget, or heal a relationship, there is a great sense of completion. Working towards

Tikkun is our natural ontological condition.

It says in the Torah that the world was created *la'asot*, 'to make' *(Genesis, 2:3)*. "To make what?" ask the sages of the Talmud. To make the world a better place, to complete creation, to make a Tikkun. Whether it is manifest in our bodies' natural way of healing itself, our obsessions with diet and health, or our passionate desire to heal the world and to make peace, it is all an expression of our yearning for Tikkun, to make right what appears to be wrong, to repair the broken.

STUDENT 1: We find this basic drive even with animals. Psychologists have discovered that animals will work to solve problems or puzzles without the incentive of any external reward. Just by virtue of their desire to solve the problem they will do so.

TEACHER: Very interesting. It is also the human longing for wholeness and integration that stimulates us to complete the creative process by bringing to life the fallen sparks hidden within everyone and everything. In doing so we are releasing these sparks, like seeds from a shell, and returning them back to their Source, thereby elevating the world to its original state of luminosity.

STUDENT 3: It is like there is a lamp that has an extension cord which is not plugged in. When we elevate the sparks of something or someone, we are plugging them back in to their Ultimate Source of Infinite Energy and connecting them back to the Light.

TEACHER: We are returning the world to its authentic self, a conscious expression of the Essence of the Creator.

STUDENT 2: Is it true that each soul has a distinct mission to locate and elevate certain sparks?

TEACHER: Yes. At times we may feel that a power beyond intellect or emotion is guiding us to do certain things, go to certain places, or meet certain people. The soul has a natural propensity to locate the sparks that it is called to elevate. The body may feel the soul's yearning for completion as an attraction to a specific person, place, or thing. This is why we have certain hungers and intuitions — they are expressions of our deepest self, our soul.

STUDENT 1: But some things that we are attracted to are not so good for us. If I'm attracted to a certain food, for example, how do I really know if it is part of my soul's mission to eat it, or if it is just a selfish craving?

TEACHER: We might think that we are attracted to the thing itself, the actual object, but it is really the spark inside it that is attracting us.
STUDENT 1: Ok, tell me more. Explain.

TEACHER: There is a life sustaining energy within all that

exists, a spark of the infinite, an eternal portion of the divine, which causes matter to live on and exist. Our purpose is to acknowledge these sparks inherent in creation and to elevate them to their original source. Each person, each soul, has the distinct mission to locate and elevate the particular sparks that he feels uniquely connected with. As such, attractions, proclivities, premonitions, and hunches are all a result of the soul's yearning to elevate the sparks contained within the physical objects the body so craves. The body feels the attraction, which emanates from the deepest reservoirs of who we are. It is then up to our mind and heart to understand the purpose of a particular desire so that we can act appropriately in order to initiate an elevation and integration of the spark back to its source.

For example, certain sparks are elevated through eating, while others are elevated through refraining. The sparks within the foods that are good for us, both spiritually and physically, are released through eating. Similarly, unhealthy foods, both spiritually unhealthy and physically unhealthy, can be elevated by not eating them. If we are attracted to something that is not good for us, we may be called to elevate those very sparks by staying away from them, by taking control of ourselves, and practicing discipline.

These sparks then achieve their highest potential in regards to our spiritual development. For if certain foods, for instance, can be seen to reach their highest potential through nourishing us in our quest to become healthier and holier people by giving us physical strength and sustenance to pray and to study and to do good deeds; then it follows that other foods reach their highest potential by strengthening our discipline and resolve in the face of unhealthy temptation. This also serves to further our quest to become holier, better people.

STUDENT 2: So while eating one food gives us physical strength, refraining from another food gives us spiritual strength.

TEACHER: Exactly. It is up to us to be able to decipher what nutrients we need at any given time.

With regards to interpersonal relationships, it is quite possible at times, that we are someone else's junk-food, or they may be ours. In such a case it may well be our self-centered and unhealthy desires for someone that may be the very obstacle standing in the way of their, or our, ultimate realization. By refraining from acting out such desires, we may in fact aid in the process of someone else's elevation by providing them with the space and time to reflect, grow, and become who they truly are. In effect, our pursuing of unhealthy desires may not only keep us down and closed off, it may also keep others down and closed off from their highest potential as well.

STUDENT 3: What if I feel a desire to over-eat and I start stuffing myself with healthy foods?

TEACHER: How does it feel? Does eating exacerbate the desire? Do you have regret after eating? Or do you have a sense of inner quiet? These can be signs of whether it was an elevation or the opposite. Clearly it is not just about what you eat, but also how you eat.

This is also true with money, which in Hebrew is *Mamon*. Mamon has a numerical value of 136, the same as the Hebrew word for ladder, *Sulam*. A ladder can stretch to heaven, but its feet are in the dirt. Money can help to feed and heal oneself or the world if it is used to elevate, or it can bring regret and chaos to oneself and to those around you if it is merely used in the service of one's more base desires and sense of instant gratification.

STUDENT 1: What if I have regrets for my past actions? Can a person elevate the sparks of their past negative behavior?

TEACHER: Absolutely. When we know that everything has holy sparks, we can look back at our past and understand that whatever happened to us was the will of the Creator — everything was meant to be. From the perspective of Unity, all is part of the Light. Everything is the way it is because of how the Light of the Creator is being revealed to us at any moment.

This even applies to what we call sin. Even a very negative act has sparks that we can elevate into positivity. In order to do this, there is a three-step process.

1. YICHUD-UNITY

The first step is *Yichud,* or Unity. This requires you to unify with, take responsibility for, and claim your mistake. Do not deny anything or defend your ego around what happened. Take ownership of your life and especially your past mistakes, and make the proper restorations.

2. BERACHA-BLESSING

The second step is *Beracha,* or Blessing. You must then attempt to view the event as a blessing. When you can see how it fits in with the larger picture you'll recognize that you were actually doing your best, given the conditions of your life at that moment. And you'll sense the divine lesson in the whole experience. This gives birth to gratitude for all the blessings we receive from the Infinite One, both hidden and revealed. Everything of your past has brought you to this moment and for that alone, everything of your past is some form of blessing. You would not be you without your past. Even if you wish to now change the course of your life, or make better decisions in the future, you are who and where you are because of your past. Your now is a truth because of then.

3. KEDUSHAH-SANCTIFICATION

The third step is *Kedushah,* Sanctification. Having first acknowledged and taken responsibility for the action, followed by perceiving it as a blessing in order to absorb its lessons, it is finally time to begin living them out. The way you think, speak, and act can now reveal the original event as essentially pure and noble. The so-called negative action was part of your path to spiritual success. The past brings you to the present.

When we turn our lives around, we can turn negative actions into merits. Not that the actions themselves change but their energy does. So instead of living out the effects of a negative past, we are able to redeem and transform the negative energy released from those past actions into a positive trajectory. We then get to live in the present with the effects of the rectified positivity of our past. This is an inner-oriented, psycho-spiritual example of elevating the fallen sparks — transforming a past misdeed into a present blessing that leads one towards greater wholeness, more expansive consciousness, and a brighter future. This is how to elevate the past.

In terms of the present and future, we still need to work, to plan, and to be ambitious in order to achieve expansiveness of spirit, nearness to the Creator, true inner contentment, and not the opposite. But in terms of the past, we need to let go and view it as being *meant to be.*

STUDENT I: It appears that the non-dual Essence includes the holy and the unholy, the shattering and the repairing. But is our mission to be dualistic in the sense that we are driven to favor the side of the holy and good, the repairing, the idea of *Tikkun?* This seems to imply that we are expressions of The Essence, but we don't act like the Essence.

TEACHER: But we do act like The Essence. This is especially clear with the third step we just mentioned. The Essence is beyond good and bad, beyond cause and effect, but that does not mean that G-d is neutral or inert. Beyond duality, is a causeless good, a good that is not in contrast to bad. With Essence consciousness, we can find the good in the bad, and elevate it. But to do this we still must be able to perceive the good and the bad — we are still required to employ discernment.

When we understand that every *Yesh* — every created thing — is an expression of the Essence, we find the harmony within the apparently chaotic world. We can find solace in the fact that there is more than meets the eye. There is a greater frame of reference, a greater context to every event.

In another sense, the Essence doesn't act at all, and yet all actions spring from the Essence. The Essence is the background set as well as the omniscient narrator of the story of Creator and creation. This story is called Torah. In it, there is a real world, with all of its difficulties and differences, and our role is to refine this world.

Everything in this real-world-story emerges with a shattering of vessels, from the chaotic birth of the entire cosmos, to the pangs and delivery of childbirth. The Torah written in our inner heart drives us to elevate the world as well as ourselves. This is our story. We are living the Divine story.

By doing Tikkun, even though everything is in essence already inherently whole, we get to write our story, to participate in the creation, to be co-creators. A parable would be of a parent hiding something very valuable from his child so that the child should look for it and find it. The desire to find, and the experience of seeking and then finding, teach the child to be more curious, creative, and responsible, as they proactively participate in their own life. This is how G-d is acting toward us.

All this hiding and seeking and shattering and healing is just so we can experience the greatest possible good. And what is the greatest possible good? The Source of all Giving and Goodness. Through helping to bring goodness into being, we ourselves become an orchestrator of goodness and giving, and as such, we enter the role as the creator, and experience the greatest possible good.

The teaching is that there is always some sliver of shame within a 'free-ride'. This is sometimes referred to as 'the bread of shame'. To truly experience the full revelation of the good we have to exert ourselves and work for it. In this way, we are taught that it is possible to view all the brokenness and suffering in our lives, and in the world, as being, in some strange and paradoxical way, only for our ultimate benefit — if only we were able to unlock its hidden potential and elevate the fallen sparks.

MEDITATION ASSIGNMENT

TEACHER: Here is your assignment for the coming week. Buy a new notebook. You're going to make brief journal entries every day, except Shabbat, which will be your day off. Take special notice of your behavior throughout each day. Briefly summarize your actions and reactions, your words, and thought patterns, in your journal. Through this writing you may begin to become aware of your patterns, your story, your narrative, and your script from a higher or more objective perspective. This journaling is an opportunity for you to become more of a writer of your own story, instead of just an unconscious character.

Look for the wisdom in everything. Everything is pointing to the Essence of Reality. Anything negative that you find or experience is merely an indicator, giving you guidelines to know where you are not yet conscious — where you can work to elevate the still fallen sparks.

Encountering yourself through journal writing, you will begin to hear your own calling, to realize your own Tikkun, and your own role in the divine world-story. And always remember: when you sense goodness, when you come to an inner quiet, this is a sign that you are elevating your sparks.

I bless you all to experience the joy of becoming who you really are.

CONVERSATION
III:

CONSCIOUSNESS

CONVERSATION III:
CONSCIOUSNESS

TEACHER: Let's begin with a story.

Rabbi Menachem Mendel of Lubavitch was orphaned from his mother at the age of three. From then on he was raised by his grandfather, Rabbi Schneur Zalman of Liadi.

One day little Menachem Mendel was sitting on his grandfather's lap. The child was pulling on the Rebbe's beard and calling: "Zeideh! Zeideh!" ('Grandpa! Grandpa!'). "But this isn't Zeideh," protested Rabbi Schneur Zalman, "this is Zeideh's beard!" So the child grabbed his grandfather's head: "This is Zeideh," he tried. "Oh no," said Rabbi Schneur Zalman "this is Zeideh's head. Where is Zeideh?"

The child pointed in turn to his Zeideh's eyes, hands, and body. "But where is Zeideh?" Rabbi Schneur Zalman kept insisting.

Suddenly, the child leaped off his grandfather's lap and ran behind the door. From his hiding place, little Mendel cried out: "ZEI-DEH!" "What is it?" called the Rebbe, turning towards the child. "Aha," exclaimed Menachem Mendel, "there's Zeideh!"

Let's leap right into contemplation today. Like the Zeideh in this story, I'm going to ask you some experiential questions. They're not meant to be merely intellectual questions, but more immediate than that. You will all need to go inside for the answers. And there are no wrong answers.

What is a human being? What are we?

Not 'Who' for the moment, but *What?* Take a look at what you are and speak from your present experience. Forget for a moment any assumptions, or anything you've ever learned.

STUDENT 1: Well… I guess I find a body here — some arms and legs. There's also some kind of abstract presence, a formless awareness, both inside and outside the body. And I am having these thoughts and perceptions. So at this moment I'd say that a human being is all of this: a spiritual being connected to a body and mind.

STUDENT 3: To me, my body gives me a sense of separation, of distinction and ego. Whereas my deeper self, lets call it my soul, gives me a sense of inter-connectivity and unity with everyone and everything around me.

TEACHER: This is true. But couldn't there be non-human beings of the same description, though perhaps lacking in the conscious awareness of separation and connectivity? What I mean is: Aren't animals also a combination of a physical body and some sort of animating energy or presence?

STUDENT 2: I think we can all admit that we normally equate a live human body/mind with a human being. So maybe we are human body/minds, enlivened by human souls.

STUDENT 3: A human being is a unity of body and soul, and mind and heart. But then again, I sense that we are more than all of these things put together. Who we really, really are has nothing to do with a bunch of parts or functions.

TEACHER: Fine. But let's move back into an experiential mode. That way we will be able to open our minds and hearts and meditate on this together. We want to discover deeper truths about who and what we really are.

Following your example, let's start by examining that which is most apparent here: the body. What is this body? We have a very habitual way of seeing bodies. And we do in fact normally identify with our body. And yet we also normally think of our bodies as opaque lumps of flesh.

Visualize this: If we were able to look at our body right now with powerful microscopic lenses we would see a vast multitude of cells firing, dancing, and working in harmony. These perpetually moving cells gather in communities to form larger units: fluids, tissues, and membranes. See how different this is from what we usually think of as a static physical human being. Only from a much wider view would we recognize this dynamic cellular galaxy as a collection of organs and limbs, a human body.

This organism, our body, has miraculously complex and so-
phisticated abilities. It feels, sees, reproduces, and repairs itself — it responds to thoughts and subconscious reflexes.

STUDENT 1: But even with all this intelligence and talent,
isn't it still basically just protoplasm, purely physical stuff?

TEACHER: Take a look right now. Does this vast network of
cells have anything to do with you? Are you made of physical tissues? If Heaven-forbid you lost an organ, or a limb,
or a function, would you still be you? If yes, then what is the
real you? If these individual ingredients do not define you,
how can the conglomeration of these ingredients define you?

If something in you insists that you are the totality of all of
your parts, what about the fact that these physical parts are
continuously being replaced? At a sub-nuclear level, the
quarks and gluons making up your body are continually
being annihilated and recreated. There's a different body
every second. On the atomic level, ninety-eight percent of
your body was not there a year ago. An organ such as the
skin is replaced every month. Your stomach lining is recreated every four days and the surface cells in the stomach that
contact food are regenerated every five minutes.

By definition, there's only one 'you' that we are looking for,
a being that experiences all of the changes and vantage

points we have just mentioned. We are looking for something that doesn't change, something that doesn't escape definition.

From another perspective, the fact that we can feel and are aware of a body confirms that we are not that body. Whatever can be observed is not the observer. You have to be separate from something in order to see it. So, if we are not our bodies, what are we? Whose body is it? Who is it that is feeling at this moment the physical sensations of the breath, the chair, the sounds coming from my mouth?

STUDENT 1: The mind is the observer of the body. I think therefore I am.

TEACHER: So perhaps I am my mind? Most people today hold the unconscious assumption that we are our minds.

But are you the collection of the thoughts that you're having? Aren't these constantly changing too? Even the brain, the repository of all the body's experiences and thoughts, is constantly changing. And when you're in deep sleep and there are no thoughts, or at least there's no observer, who are you then?

In truth we project our own reality. Nothing exists, including 'myself', unless I think about it. In that sense, I am my mind. But it is interesting to note that we say 'my mind,' because we can observe the mind. Who is it that observes the mind?

Does the mind observe the mind? There are many levels within the mind. A deeper level of the mind can converse with another level of the mind. And there are still deeper levels of mind that experience that inner conversation.

Let us enter meditation more deeply for a few minutes.

Quiet yourself for a moment. Watch your thoughts. You may be thinking about how to follow these instructions or do this meditation. Or you may be distracted by something and your thoughts are wandering. Instead of trying to focus or push away your thoughts, just let them be where and what they are. Then ask: Who is it that allows these thoughts to be here? Who or what is the 'space' in which these thoughts are occurring? And now: Who is asking? Who is it that searches for the answer? Who is it that looks for the one who searches for the answer? Who, or what, is the space in which this looking occurs? Now stop looking for an answer. Just stay open and let the questions resonate, without the need for an answer: Who am I...? What am I...?

(Long silence... a sigh)

STUDENT 3: I am the silence of the non-answer.

TEACHER: Interesting. And in this moment, now that you're creating sounds and giving us an answer, who are you?

STUDENT 3: Well, I'm no longer silent in the same way. But it seems like my words are coming out of a silent space.

TEACHER: Not that this is the final answer yet, but the traditional name for this silence is *Chaya*, or Life Force, one of the 5 levels of our soul. Everything else comes and goes, but the I, *Ani*. Ani is not identified with either the body or the mind and yet observes it both. Ani is the eternal, infinite soul.

The soul is not contained by space or time. It is separate from all outer influences or identifications. It is the I that was there when you were young and said, "I am young". And it is the same I that was there when you grew a bit older and said, "I am old." It is the totality of little Menachem Mendel's Zeideh.

STUDENT 2: So far, I think the true I sounds like the Essential Self that we have been discussing. I understand that Ani is ultimately what I am, but does this make sense? Isn't Essence impersonal?

TEACHER: The Essence is also an individual personal I. The Essence is everything. It does not erase individuality.

STUDENT 1: It sounds like you're saying that my soul is unique to me, whereas Ani is the essence of everything and everyone. So are we talking about two different ranges along a spectrum of the same reality?

TEACHER: There are paradoxes here. Let me clarify, without getting too into semantics. First, remember that Ani is not a thing, it is not a part of you, and you are not a part of It.

It does not have parts or boundaries.

Second, we sometimes refer to the soul as 'my soul', as if it is something we possess. To be totally clear: We don't 'have' a soul — we are the soul. The soul incorporates all levels of being from the superficial egoic personality associated with the body and mind, to higher and more-subtle spiritual manifestations of our self.

The context and inseparable essence of this manifestation is Ani. Essence and manifestation are inseparable. Yet, we don't want to confuse them. 'I' am not Essence. I am an expression of the Essence called Soul.

STUDENT I: Let me understand this. Is there an individual I? Or is the I a simple illusion? Are we all the same in our Essence or different?

TEACHER: We are all different, we are not the same, and we are all unique. Every individual person, every parcel of life or moment of time, is utterly unique. We are all distinct expressions of the Ultimate I. The self is not an illusion, nor is it a mirage, and the objective of a spiritual life is not to surrender our particularity, our uniqueness, our story, our heritage, but rather to celebrate our uniqueness — who we are and what we uniquely contribute.

Sameness is Ayin, empty of all form. Uniqueness is an expression of *Atzmut*, Essence. This is true equality: different and equal, celebrating our, and everyone else's, uniqueness. By securing a healthy sense of self-worth, a person can be truly open to sense another person's worth and uniqueness as well.

From the perspective of *Yesh*, one person is pitted against the next and it is either you or me. This perspective creates strife between people, as well as between people and their environment. From the perspective of *Ayin*, there is no longer an 'us' or a 'them', we are all the same.

Yet, from the deepest perspective our uniqueness still exists. The unity between Yesh and Ayin is that the ego exists but is completely transparent. This means that there is a strong sense of selfhood and a total awareness of the selfhood of others. This is a paradigm of you and me, us and them.

Now let's look deeper into what we mean by the word Soul.

ANATOMY OF THE SOUL

Earlier we said that the observer and the observed are by definition separate. Yet, there is a level of soul where knowledge, knower, and knowing are all one. This means that in its deepest, most pristine point the soul is one with the Infinite Unity. It is rooted in Oneness, yet it also emanates and becomes distinct. Still sparkling with the light of the Infinite, the soul descends through various levels into a particular human embodiment. A soul is like a holographic

particle of the Infinite, and yet it is also finite in its proper-
ties and expression. Every soul has a unique spiritual voca-
tion to be fulfilled on earth.

STUDENT 2: I don't understand how something can be both
finite and infinite?

TEACHER: It is a profound paradox. The brain cannot really
grasp it. Let's leave it at this: The soul can be both finite and
infinite because it is an expression of the Essence which
maintains and is manifest in both the finite world as well as
Infinity.

STUDENT 3: Is the emanation of our soul analogous to *Hishtalshelut,* the hierarchical chain of the inner worlds?

TEACHER: Yes. The word Hishtalshelut refers to the cosmic
unfolding, from Infinity all the way to finite reality. It also
refers to the soul's descent to the physical world. This
process is mirrored and mapped within our own consciousness and creative process.

Our soul is the vehicle that allows us to ascend to those
higher, inner realities. It is through those deeper realities,
that we connect all the way back to the Source of all life.
Just like a candle flame flickers and reaches upwards, the
soul, which is called 'the candle of Hashem,' reaches with
deep yearning toward its Source. Let us trace the ascending
light of this candle flame.

Intellectual study can bring us to the door — the threshold of spiritual awakening — but the soul itself is the key to unlocking and entering these higher, deeper, subtler realms. So I invite you again to allow these contemplative words to evoke for you the realities they describe.

(The teacher lights a candle)

FIVE EXPRESSIONS OF SOUL

1. NEFESH:

TEACHER: The bottom of the candle flame, the blue part next to the wick, is the part of the soul that is the least conscious of its Source.

This level of the soul is referred to as *Nefesh*. Nefesh is the animating element and intelligence of the physical body, organizing the cells of the body and all its functions, instincts, and sensory experiences. Because it articulates and forms the existence of the body, Nefesh is symbolized by the mouth. As the Creator speaks creation into being, our Nefesh is the mouthpiece through which our physical body is spoken into being.

Nefesh is associated with the *Sefira* of *Malchut*, receptiveness, royalty and kingship, which although on the bottom of the Tree of Life, is also associated with the mouth. This reveals the principle that words can create worlds and that true authority is manifest through one's power of speech. King David, the sweet singer of Israel and author of the Psalms, is also associated with the Sefira of Malchut.

Blockage in this level of soul is evident when our base instincts and appetites are exacerbated through addictive or reactive habits. Imbalances often manifest as a sense of heaviness, self-destructive habits, or a general resistance to life.

Tune in to your Nefesh right now. Ask yourself: On this level, Who am I? What's my job? What do I really want?

STUDENT 1: I want to eat. I'm hungry.

TEACHER: Good…anything else?

STUDENT 3: Actually, I really want to feel love.

TEACHER: Ok, let's think about love for a moment. What is more fulfilling, when someone loves you, or when you offer a loving act or gesture to someone else?

STUDENT 2: When I do something for someone else.

TEACHER: Yes, and this altruistic act will bring your consciousness to a higher and deeper level, for example the next aspect of soul.

2. RUACH:

TEACHER: Ascending the candle flame, we come to *Ruach*, the warm glow in the middle.

Ruach is subtler than physicality. It represents the dimension of emotions, creative self-expression, and devotional spirituality. When you are moved by beautiful music, for example, or a kind act, you are stimulating the faculties of Ruach. Ruach is internal movement. The meaning of the word Ruach is 'Wind' or 'Breath'. Therefore it is associated with the nose.

Ruach is connected to the *Sefira* of *Tiferet*, Beauty or Compassion, and is represented by the patriarch Yaakov. Let us look at the story of Yaakov falling in love with Rachel, apparently on account of her beauty. There was something much deeper going on between these two cosmic characters then Yaakov being physically attracted to Rachel's beauty, but it took his marriage to her sister Leah and seven additional years of intense work to be able to properly elevate the sparks of Rachel's physical beauty without getting stuck there as an end in itself. This would not have served either Yaakov or Rachel in their mission to become who they truly were.

Misaligned Ruach is when we get stuck on beauty. Rather than praising the Author of the beauty, we make the beauty itself into an idol, an object of devotion. Beauty then becomes an end in itself, instead of an associative trigger or vehicle to connect us to the Source of that Beauty. This is, in effect, how the initial Sefirot shattered, as explored earlier. They were all ends in themselves. They lost the context of their existence and in turn, their connection to a greater purpose and structure of which they were a part. They confused their individual parts for the whole.

Let your heart open to this level of consciousness now. I'm speaking to you at the level of Ruach: Who are you? What is your purpose?

STUDENT 3: My purpose, from a place of Ruach, is to elevate awareness through joy.

TEACHER: And what might be the purpose of that joy?

STUDENT 3: I don't think of it as having a purpose, but you mentioned music. When we gather to pray together and the prayers are sung joyfully, I go into in a mildly altered state and the words feel more meaningful and uplifting. Music can also bring me out of a sense of depression and when I'm happier, I make better choices in life. That could be a purpose, if there is one.

TEACHER: Thank you. That brings us to the next aspect of soul...

3. NESHAMA

TEACHER: The light at the top of the candle, the white edge of the flame, is *Neshama*.

Neshama represents higher intellect and spiritual wisdom. When Neshama is our context, intellect becomes a truth unto itself and intelligence is revered no matter where it leads. When it is aligned with the Source, Neshama is the power to choose, to consciously co-create our reality. This is where human language and meaning resides. It is linked with the *Sefira* of *Bina*, or Understanding. Understanding is likened hearing, and so Neshama is also linked with the ears.

Nefesh, Ruach and Neshama constitute normative consciousness. Living integrated and harmonious with these amazing tools and faculties gives us the opportunity to climb higher and deeper into the Tree of Life. Kabbalah seeks to develop the perspective of inclusive transcendence, meaning that we do not cut ourselves off from the lower levels when we go to a higher one. A person with elevated understanding can, and should, still have emotions and healthy physical functioning.

So Neshama: Who are you? Where do you lead?

STUDENT 1: I am the pathway to and from Divine intellect. When I draw Divine intellect into the mind, I awaken insight. Insight illuminates our thoughts, words, and actions, energizing us to be in alignment with our deepest self.

TEACHER: Excellent!

4. & 5. CHAYA & YECHIDA

TEACHER: Nefesh, Ruach, and Neshama represent our normative consciousness. They are our capacities for deepening and expanding our lives. They influence the body/heart/mind, and in turn the body/heart/mind can influence them. As a person matures spiritually, generally Nefesh unfolds first, then Ruach, and then Neshama; although there are rare instances when this progression occurs in a different order.

Chaya and *Yechida* are not really capacities, nor are they parts of the candle flame. They are levels of soul that encircle the human being from above, so to speak. They transcend the individual awareness and personality and they are beyond the influence of the body/heart/mind. At the same time, they permeate and include all the other levels.

Chaya is called *Makif Ha'karov*, the Close Encircling. *Chaya* means life. We experience and express Chaya as an inner will. Will is the drive that transforms dreams into reality. Will is the prevailing force of the entire cosmos.

STUDENT 2: There are many kinds of will, aren't there? The will to beat the lines at the department store, the will to survive at any cost, the will to wake up from spiritual slumber…

TEACHER: The innermost will of the human being is to be in sync with the will of the Creator. The Creator's will is the foundation of all reality. It is the deepest truth and purpose of all creation. Chaya is the interface between human will and Divine will.

STUDENT 1: Since Chaya transcends individual awareness, I guess we cannot consciously understand what the Divine will is? But then how do we express and experience Chaya as will?

TEACHER: Neshama corresponds to the cognitive experience of understanding. Chaya is beyond that. In a sense, it could be glimpsed as a subtle, intuitive understanding beyond intellectual limits. We do not really have to understand something in order to interface with it. We are now ascending beyond understanding altogether.

Chaya is associated with the *Sefira* of *Chochmah*, Wisdom. This Sefira is a precursor to *Bina*, Understanding, and is likened to sudden lightning like flashes of inspiration or insight, as if coming out of nowhere. The key to Chochmah is to be open and receptive to these Divine Flashes and then to keep the energy, information, and inspiration moving through the chain of being. The key to Bina is to quiet down enough to really listen to what is being communicated. Chochmah is seeing — the ability to receive the signal. Bina is listening — the capacity to process and contextualize the transmission.

STUDENT 3: And what is Yechida?

TEACHER: Yechida is called *Makif Ha'rachok*, the Distant Encircling. *Yechida*, means Unique or Oneness. It is the self that is one with the Infinite. It is the Infinite space upon which the finite expressions of soul are projected.

Yechida cannot be quantified or contextualized. We cannot observe, understand, or experience Yechida, because it is one with the Observer, the Understander, and the Ultimate Experiencer. Yet, for the sake of our discussion we will consider Yechida to be the clearest expression of our true self, since it is the last answer we can have to the question: "Who am I?" Yechida is the big uninfluenced, unchanging I, within which we live out our small 'i' experiences.

STUDENT I: But, the way Yechida is being described sounds a lot like Essence — the space in which we live out our small 'i' experiences. The difference is that now we are calling Yechida a level, and before you had established that Essence is really beyond level or hierarchy.

TEACHER: That is correct. We have said that Essence is not a separate thing, not even a separate thing that is beyond all hierarchy. It is beyond the 'beyond'. Yechida is the unity between the soul and the Creator — the two that are really one. Essence is not about that kind of unity. Essence is one that is really One.

Yechida is referred to as *Makif Ha'rachok* since within it, so to speak, there is a *Nitzutz Boreh*, a Spark of the Creator, as well as a *Nitzutz Nivrah*, a Spark of Creation. In other words, Yechida is the interface with the Infinite Source. It is both a level and not a level.

It is valid to question the meaning of so-called distance or *Rachok*, in relation to Yechida. Yechida actually permeates all the other levels, including Nefesh. It is not distant, it is here and now. Living consciously on the level of Yechida is an extremely high spiritual level. In that state, one's thoughts, words, and deeds are in perfect harmony with the Creator and with creation. One sees every level of oneself and all beings for what they really are — nothing other than an expression of the Divine. At the same time, one is also very down to earth and in touch with physical reality.

STUDENT 3: Can you please give me a metaphor so I can wrap my mind around this idea?

TEACHER: Sure. Think in terms of an ocean and waves. If the Infinite One, the source of all souls, could be compared to an endless ocean — and remember do not take this metaphor literally — the Yechida could be compared to the water. Chaya would be the rushing current and deep movement of the waters. Neshama, Ruach and Nefesh would each be different parts of an individual wave. The initial up surge and ideal form of the wave as a whole would be the Neshama. The swelling rise of the waters to actually become that wave, as envisioned and initiated by the Neshama, would be the Ruach. And the whitecap on the crest of the wave would be the Nefesh. From the perspective of the ocean, the wave is indistinguishable from itself. From the perspective of the tumultuous whitecap (Nefesh), you feel yourself to be at a distance from the ocean, as if you are an independent entity. The deeper regions of the wave, Ruach and certainly Neshama, can see more easily that they are not, in any way, separate from the ocean.

Each wave has its own distinct personality, which is a genuine reality on its own level. Although focusing only on the personality could cause one to forget one's true water-nature. Yet water is water, within every level, including the level of the ocean itself. In this sense there are no separate levels. This is why we can say that the soul is who we really are. There is only water.

One of the ways this wave analogy breaks down is that souls do not just disappear back into the Ocean with no effect. Every soul is a unique spiritual force, even in the after-life, and the returning wave, after manifesting for a number of years in this world as the soul of a particular human being, returns back into the ocean. It still retains its distinct wave quality. The lifetime in the body therefore takes on great importance, for now and for all eternity.

STUDENT 1: Do we really ascend or descend through different levels just by discussing or meditating on them?

TEACHER: Some levels we may ascend or descend by speaking about them, some by meditating, and some by doing. Ultimately our goal is to travel life's paths with our thoughts, speech, and actions all aligned as one harmonious trajectory of conscious energy. So, yes it is possible to ascend or descend through certain levels simply by speech or meditation.

Our awareness corresponds to how we have chosen to live. Generally we ascend from one rung to the next, although sometimes we skip over levels only to fall back later to where we have stabilized. Basically it is our choice whether we live from the surface or from the depths. Meditation can help focus our faculty of free choice.

THE BODY

STUDENT 3: Don't we have to dis-identify to some extent from the body, so we can identify with the depths of our spiritual self?

TEACHER: This is a very important question, one that the great masters of Kabbalah have wrestled with throughout history. True, we are a soul, but soul does not exclude the body. Let us try to understand the body as deeply as possible.

First, let us see how the Kabbalistic view of the body developed over time. There were three periods in this development:

1. The first was the era before R. Isaac Luria, the Ari.
2. Then there was the period inspired by the Ari.
3. The third period — our current era — is inspired by the teachings of the Baal Shem Tov.

STUDENT 3: So we are getting progressively deeper and deeper into the body?

TEACHER: Yes, time does not only flow in one direction. The present is being pulled by the future as much as it is being pushed by the past. In matters of spirituality, as we move through history, closer to the era of universal Redemption, deeper and deeper truths are being revealed.

This is also valid with regards to our relationship with the body. This deeper understanding occurs for two reasons. First, we have an increasing need for these deeper truths. There has never been such widespread obsession with the body and at the same time, disconnection from the truths of the body. Secondly, the closer we are moving towards our collective Redemption, the more we get tastes of *Olam Haba*, the Future World, in the present. The future world will be a heaven-on-earth experienced in physical bodies, as Nachmonides *(13th century)* writes. Everyone will have full Yechida consciousness integrated within their individual psychophysical awareness.

STUDENT 2: Are these three periods related at all with the three perspectives we have explored earlier?

TEACHER: Yes, very good. These three periods reflect the three paradigms of Divinity, which we have already explored in detail:

1. Finite
2. Infinite
3. Essence

They also reflect the three world-views we have discussed:

A. *Ilah* and *Alul* — a worldview of cause and effect.
B. *Tzimtzum* — a worldview of concealment and contraction.
C. *Tzimtzum Lo K'pshuto* — an Essence world-view in which G-d's concealment and contraction is understood to be not literal.

EARLY PERIOD

In the early period, the prevailing idea was to neglect the physical to reach the spiritual.

The great 11th century moralist *R. Bachya Ibn Pekudah* writes in his magnum opus, "Duties of the Heart," that the body is a prison for the soul. The *Chasidei Ashkenaz*, the Pious Ascetics of Old Germany, most prominently expressed these ideas during the 12th and 13th centuries. To rectify wrongdoing done with the body they would roll in snow during winter, or lay covered in worms during the summer. Numerous and extended fasts were the path to atonement and personal and cosmic *Tikkun*.

This approach served a valid purpose within its era. In a moment we will discuss why it is no longer appropriate.

In the first worldview, the spiritual soul is a cause and its effect is the body. If you have this view, your natural attitude is: "Why engage the body at all when I can tap into the cause? Why get involved in the bottom of the devolving chain when I can ascend to a higher level?"

Since cause and effect are relative and seemingly mutually exclusive, you tend to opt for one over the other. You then begin to neglect the body in order to reach the soul. This was also expressed in the way that people would gorge and indulge the body in a display of anti-spirituality — pure animalistic physicality. So you can see that on both sides of the debate there was a strong dichotomy being expressed. This was the way the body was understood before the teachings of the Ari were revealed to the world.

THE PERIOD OF THE ARI

STUDENT 2: And what did the Ari reveal?

TEACHER: In the next era, deeper levels of insight were revealed. The Ari and the other profound teachers of the city of Sefad taught that under certain conditions the body could be utilized on the spiritual path. The body therefore gains validity and purpose from a spiritual perspective. Rather than neglecting the body, you can use it as a vehicle for the soul, *L'sheim Shamayim*, For the Sake of Heaven.

The Ari's *Tzimtzum* teaching allows for a radical and qualitative leap from *Ayin,* or nothingness, to *Yesh*, somethingness. The Infinite has made room for a finite existence. What is the meaning of this? Why would the Ayin create something else?

STUDENT 3: Good question, why would the Infinite make room for and create the finite?

TEACHER: Love. Love makes room for an other. Creation is an act of love. The sole purpose of the existence of an other is to experience a re-unification with the One.

According to this perspective the body has a purpose. It is not an obstacle to be excluded. The body is an expression of the Creator, designed to be an instrument for reunification with the Beloved. The natural response to this view is not to fast, but to eat in order to pray better and to sleep in order to have more strength to study and meditate and to do more good deeds and acts of kindness.

THE PERIOD OF THE BAAL SHEM TOV

STUDENT 2: And today, what do we understand?

TEACHER: With the Baal Shem Tov an unprecedented awakening took place. He introduced the concept of the Essential self, that which embraces all the levels of manifestation. In other words, he emphasized love. Our true nature is love. We naturally love all people because we are of one Essence. This is our natural state, unless impeded through conflict or trauma, we are naturally loving and open to connect.

When the Baal Shem met his first real student, the *Toldos*, he told him to "stop tugging on the reigns". He was explaining to be easy with the body. Do not hold on too tight or tug to hard. It is precisely by letting go a little bit, that the body can run faster and further.

The body is our vehicle of transportation through life. We need to treat it with respect and care, and we need to include it within our journey of spiritual development. As our spirit is a manifestation of the Infinity of Essence, our bodies are a manifestation of the finitude of Essence.

Excessive fasting harms the body. The Baal Shem Tov taught, "A small wound in the body is a large wound in the spirit". Taking care of the body is taking care of the soul. Rather than learning how to fast, or even how to eat for some transcendent purpose, we are given the opportunity to learn to eat with a deeper consciousness.

The act of eating itself can be a transformative and noble experience if done with true *Kavanah,* or Intention. Thus eating and other bodily acts are not only valuable as necessary pre-cursors to a future *Mitzvah* or meditation, but through our elevated awareness, these bodily acts are able to become spiritual activities in and of themselves. Not eating in order to meditate, but eating *as meditation*.

Since Tzimtzum is not literal, and everything is an expression of and contained within the Creator, the body, therefore, is also sacred; not merely as a vehicle to serve the soul, but as a sacred entity unto itself. When we become aware of our Unity with the Creator intimately through our physical actions, we actualize this sacredness in every moment of life.

If the Tzimtzum were a literal reality, the body would be just a created thing, infinitely removed from the Creator. But with no literal separation, there is no literally separate body. What we call the physical is simply an expression of the Light of the Creator within finitude, as physicality.

Spiritual maturity emerges as one comes to the realization that the body is not a jailhouse for the soul, although of course it can be in the earlier stages of spiritual development. Then, the naturally transcendent soul opens up to include the body and the body offers the transcendent soul the opportunity to experience the finite world — otherwise known as G-d's Creation. Expressing our self on all levels, we become fully aware of the Unity between our individual I and the Ultimate I.

THE PATH OF LOVE

TEACHER: The implication of the path of the Baal Shem Tov is love. The book of Proverbs teaches, "In all your ways you shall know Him." 'In all your ways…' means, in every aspect of life we should strive to know, to cleave to, and to be one with the Creator, with 'Him'.

'Him' in the Hebrew language is the word *Hu*, which is spelled as Hei, Vav (הו). These are also the last two letters of the four-letter name of the Infinite One and they correspond to the level of Divinity that descends into finitude. 'To know' means to have an intimate knowing. Thus this passage means, "Be intimate with your Creator in all aspects of your life." Let every thing you do reveal Hashem's love into the world.

The spreading outward of love begins with healthy self-esteem and self-love. Selfish self-love is a lack of self-esteem, it is not true love at all. Those who truly love reflect the Creator, the Source of Love. The Infinite One created space for the finite universe with all its variety and abundance. To emulate the Creator is to give others the space to be themselves. We have to start by also giving ourselves this necessary space to be who we truly are.

Then we can emanate our love outwardly to family, friends, and to all people. This love for others can become ecstatic — almost maddening. There are no obstacles, for all are embraced within the One.

Love is the functioning of our essential nature. Our primary motivation in life is love, to reveal apparent duality as Oneness. Even all of our physical desires are for Unity. Nothing else can give us true lasting satisfaction.

STUDENT 2: To me, this path seems so much more positive, wholesome and joyful than the previous models.

TEACHER: We all need to look and see if our spirituality is up to date. Do we still give some credence, even subconsciously, to the paradigm of unworthiness, punishment, and rejection? When we make a mistake, do we blame ourselves and then simply wallow in our guilt, or do we take responsibility for our past action, and then look for the good in ourselves and build on that?

If you notice a fault with someone else, turn inward and ask yourself: "Why am I seeing this?" The other is your mirror reflecting back to you the work that you need to do. Instead of fasting to atone, or rejecting your mistakes, you can learn from your mistakes. Everything and everyone in your life appears for the sake of your spiritual development.

Here is a meditation from the Baal Shem Tov that you can bring into daily life:

When you speak with a person, at home or in the street, focus on the fact that you are now having a conversation with the Creator through this person. The Creator is sending you a message and telling you something at this very moment. Ask yourself: "What is the message?" There is a message for you in the words that the other is saying.

At the same time do not, of course, ignore their surface self, do not devalue or exclude any part of the person. Just like you, they represent the whole spectrum of cosmos and consciousness. The waves are not separate from the ocean. There is no separate other. There is only One I. Ein od mil'-vado, 'There is nothing but G-d'.

AFTERWORD

TEACHER: I want to thank you all for coming out in the middle of the night to study these precious teachings. You were all completely present and necessary to help bring out each facet of this shimmering diamond that we call True Existence. Hopefully we are all a little bit better equipped to see the Light hidden within this diamond, as well as the Hand that continuously forms it from nothing.

In order to bring about this subtle shift in consciousness it was essential for us to excavate our own minds, hearts, bodies, and souls so as to get a clearer picture of true reality, as opposed to how it was previously determined by the confines of our limited consciousness. This work is never-ending. These conversations are merely an opening. You must continue to walk through the doors and gates as you encounter them. The path is the purpose. *Enjoy.*

I have included below a short synopsis of the topics that were covered over the course of these classes. It is my sincerest wish that you find it helpful to summarize and situate this multi-dimensional material within an overall unified structure.

◨

SYNOPSIS

KABBALAH

Kabbalah is not theology in the strict sense of the word. Theology implies the Creator and the created, as if they are separate. Kabbalah comes to dispel this notion. Neither is it, strictly speaking, a mystical branch of thought. Mysticism implies the fallacy of our empirical perception and sense experiences. In such a perspective there is no creation, the mystic is ascetic and un-attached. Kabbalah asks us to trust our senses, and yet to sense the depths within — to live within the world and yet to not feel trapped by it.

Kabbalah is referred to as The Tree of Life. Throughout this dialogue we have explored the three fundamental facets of our lives:

> 1) The Source of our being
> 2) The Place of our being
> 3) The Purpose of our being.

In other words: Creator, Creation and Consciousness.

Only after we wrestle with and secure a better understanding of the above-mentioned aspects of our experience can we begin to understand the Kabbalistic worldview of life from the personal, the collective, and the cosmic purpose.

Ultimately, the journey of life should make us *more* not less, *expansive* not constrictive, *joyful* not depressed. It should fill us with a renewed sense of gratitude and appreciation for the beauty of all that life contains.

THE CREATOR

The *Ohr Ein Sof* or Infinite Light, is a Unified Whole, and yet when we look around we see multiplicity, duality, up and down, right and left, past and future. The question is: Why? Why do we see duality and multiplicity if all is One?

On all levels of existence multiplicity seems to be the operative term. Time appears to flow from a by-gone past into the fleeting present, impregnating a distant future. Space functions within clear and fixed dimensions. History, superficially observed, seems to be a great unfolding of unrelated events and loosely strung together episodes. Psychologically, we tend to view our inner experience as a constant battle between various forces within us. Because of this it seems that if we are not busy warring within ourselves or between each other, then we are collectively warring against our environment or some other abstract threat.

Creation is not a process of converting pure energy or infinite spirit into reified, finite, contextualized matter. But rather, creation occurs through a great quantum leap, a *Tzimtzum,* or Contraction, of the light within itself. So while there was, and is, only the Ohr Ein Sof, in order to create space for otherness and apparent separation there was a Tzimtzum of the Infinite Light that allowed finite otherness to come into focus.

We have the divine-like power to create, but to do so we need to blend it with a properly applied practice of Tzimtzum, of contraction and holding back. The most beautiful of creations is that which emerges from the union of two people. Healthy relationships with others are founded on the balance between expanding and sharing, and contracting and listening. Learn to speak properly, but also learn to listen, and listen deeply. The greatest gift we can offer another is to listen to them and allow them to be who they truly are.

Initially, the otherness took shape as an undifferentiated potential containing the possibility for all eventual, individuated life. And then slowly a line was formed with distinct points and a defined structure, with a clear beginning and a definite end.

The original points along this line are the first set of ten Sefirot.

These are the kaleidoscopic screens through which the infinite light penetrates our reality. These distinctly formed, shaped, and colored vessels serve as curtains or colored containers through which the Infinite, Colorless, Formless, and Unified Light is refracted and reflected into our world.

The order of the Sefirot is as follows:

First there is the initial will and desire to create:
KETER
Crown, Faith, Will: Super-Conscious

Next are the intellectual Sefirot:
CHOCHMAH: Wisdom and Intuition
BINA: Understanding and Reason

Next are the three primary internal emotions:
On the right, expansive column is
CHESED: Loving-Kindness and Giving.
On the left, restrictive column is
GEVURA: Strength and Restraint.
In the middle is their synthesis,
TIFERET: Beauty and Compassion.

This triad represents the dynamic of the giver giving with a conscious sensitivity towards the needs of the receiver.

The outer emotions are also divided into three:
On the right, expansive column is
NETZACH: Victory and Perseverance.
On the left column is
HOD: Acknowledgment and Humility.
In the middle is the unifying agent, connecting the giver
and the receiver,
YESOD: Foundation and Connection.

And finally, on the bottom is
MALCHUT: Royalty and Receptiveness.

Malchut represents the vessel that receives from the preceding nine Sefirot and re-channels the energies downward, thus becoming the *Keter,* or Crown, for the subsequent structure of Sefirot. Conversely, Malchut also channels the energies upward back to the Source from which they came.

So, while the Light is one and formless, when that Light is projected into our reality it appears as differentiated and colored. This is descriptive of the Creator and creation. The Creator is One, but through the creative process, the Infinite Unity is channeled, reflected, and refracted through the cosmic energy transformers known as the Sefirot.

Through this process the One Light is manifest in this world via the particular qualities and attributes of the Sefirot. This is why we can discern Hashem's attributes in the world such as mercy, compassion, strength, love, judgment, and so forth.

So for instance, when we delve deeply into the mystery of creation we are able to observe the *Chochmah* of *Ohr Ein Sof,* or when we sit and watch the sunset over the horizon we can get a glimpse of the *Tiferet* of *Ohr Ein Sof,* as it were. It is All One Light, just manifesting through different vessels.

When life seems difficult and you are observing the Light as reflected through the *Sefira* of *Gevura* — withholding and restrictiveness — remember that there is only One. Everything we experience in life is a reflection of The One and ultimately the One creates out of love. Find the hidden spark, connect with it, and elevate it.

Yet, because the instrument of our understanding is our brain — a binary apparatus by its very existence — the image we have of the Ohr Ein Sof in its pure nature is that it is detached and transcendent. Pure formless light is beyond creation and what we can appreciate is merely the rays of the infinite light reflected within our finite world. What we perceive is manifestation, not Essence.

And yet, the primary book of Kabbalah, the Zohar, teaches: "There is no thought that can grasp You, but You can be grasped by the arousal of the heart." The metaphor of the heart is indicative of a kind of non-brain, an alternative to our intellect's inherently dualistic perception. The heart beckons us to a more integrated and deeply felt awareness. The image of *Ohr,* Light, being separate from or higher then the *Kli* or Vessel, is merely another construct of duality and separateness. In the world of absolute Unity there is only One, and both infinite light and finite vessels are simply manifestations of The One. This Oneness is referred to as *Etzem* or *Atzmut*, Pure Essence: that which is present within the finite, but also beyond the infinite. Etzem is beyond even the definition of being the source of the infinite.

Essence is inclusive transcendence. It is beyond all expression and is thus able to contain all expressions, even those that seem contradictory and paradoxical. We are not speaking of pantheism, for although the world is a divine expression, it is not the totality of Essence. In the words of the ancient sages, "He (G-d) is the place of the universe, but the universe is not His place."

All of reality is the expression of essence. Clearly, there are no separate practices or meditations on essence because essence is not a separate phenomenon on which we can meditate. In this sense we cannot be aware of essence. We can only be essence. When we live in this condition we live in alignment and unity with ourselves, with our Creator, with our community, with our environment, and with the entire created reality.

CREATION

All creation, referred to as *Yesh*, is an expression of essence, referred to as *Yesh Amiti* or True Existence. Being that reality is a manifestation of the Real, it too is real. The universe, along with all of its potential and manifest energy, is a radiant expression of absolute oneness.

The uniqueness of physicality in the spiritual scheme of creation is that it lives according to the illusion that it is self-referential and independent of a Source or Creator. Yet, from a more expansive state of awareness, this physical reality does not exist the way we may perceive it as separate and autonomous. Rather, it is merely another expression of the all-encompassing, all-pervading Essence.

In our mind's perception, for the infinite light to appear as a finite vessel, for oneness to manifest as many, there first needs to be a *Tzimtzum*, a contraction and concealment.

Creation occurs through a shattering and this process is replicated throughout all creation. Every creative act is brought about through a course of shattering. From birth on the macrocosmic level, commonly referred to as the big bang, to birth on a microcosmic level, such as in the birth of a child, all creation ensues with a process of concealment, gestation, and shattering. We can witness this shattering in the often-violent pangs of a mother as she gives birth to a beautiful new life.

But even in our day-to-day life experiences, every new moment begins with a Tzimtzum of sorts, a withdrawal from the past in order to create the new. And we must accordingly shatter the static status quo of reality in order to interject something novel or unexpected. This idea of shattering is also represented by smashing the glass at a wedding. This is the last act of the ceremony and accordingly it ushers in a new creation, a new state of being, a new life.

On a cosmic level, first there is one, which excludes the two. Then a Tzimtzum occurs, which gives rise to two-ness and duality. Our cosmic, collective, and personal purpose is realized when we integrate the two back within the One.

Tikkun, or Fixing, Elevation, and Repair, is achieved when we recognize the divine sparks of Unity within all of the multiplicity, within all of creation. Now, having achieved a Tikkun, the Unity does not exclude the two, but rather gathers the two within its transcendent embrace.

Our innate ontological condition and drive is geared towards Tikkun. This natural way of being is manifest in our body's innate and organic capacity to heal itself, in our passionate desire to fix the world at large, and within our drive to spiritually re-integrate the disparate and somewhat schizophrenic drives within ourselves.

There have been many perspectives posited as the ultimate and underlying motivating factor of human consciousness. Some have defined the motivating factor of human life as one's libido, while others have posited a collective consciousness that is manifest through archetypal dreams and mythic aspirations. There have also been those who have determined that it is the Will and quest for power that is the ultimate drive, while still others speak of self-actualization. In truth, unity is our primary motivating factor, the notion of transforming two into one. This powerful innate desire to re-unify with the infinite light is the underlying drive of all desires, and nothing will give us satisfaction — no object, subject, gadget, or even person — until we realize this truth.

We all seek Tikkun to repair and bring the world of many back into One. We all desire unity. We all crave relationships or experiences that bring two together into a condition of One. Sadly, this primordial and spiritual force, when undirected, compels us to buy more shoes then we need or consume more food than desired, for example. Walking around with a deep sense of emptiness, as we desire to feel connected, we erroneously assume that if we reach out to possess the newest version of the 'i-Pad', or to buy the latest model SUV, we will feel more connected and satisfied. But of course it never lasts. It is like trying to patch up a deep psychological trauma with a band-aid. It is like trying to put a piece of fruit back onto a tree. In truth, we must become the tree in order to bear fresh fruit.

We all seek unity, within ourselves and with others. One being alone is similar to the Infinite One prior to creation. This was a state of absolute oneness, excluding all otherness. But now life is about relationships, bringing two together into one. Whether it is a relationship with other people, places, or things, when we understand the spiritual nature of our attractions, a deeper relationship is forged. Everything in our life then, all of the twos, are included within the transcendent context of Unity.

Life is not about simple refraining or denial, as mortifying the flesh can be as addictive as pampering it, and fasting from food, for example, can show an attachment to food as indulging. Everything in life is a divine expression and should be appreciated as such. Everything in our lives whether people, places, objects, or subjects can and should be included within such Ultimate Unity. This is the way we achieve our Tikkun and become spiritually satisfied.

Our unique purpose and Tikkun is fulfilled when we are truly honest with ourselves, when we are fully aware of our strengths and pursue them, and when we are equally attuned to our weaknesses and aspire to overcome them. Write a daily journal, or mentally review your day before retiring to bed and observe your strengths and weaknesses.

Practically speaking, the notion of merging two into one translates as such: In order for us to reach our own personal Tikkun, which will empower us to catalyze a cosmic Tikkun, we need to be fully honest with ourselves. We need to uncover what our unique 'two' is all about so we can express the infinite unity within our own diversity. Simply put, this means consciously following the patterns of your life, whether mentally through meditation, or creatively through writing a journal. You must take the time and put forth the effort to recognize and realize your true gift of genius. You will then truly know your strong points and passions in order to pursue them and bring them to fruition. You must also put forth the effort to take account of yourself and notice your weaknesses and challenges, the areas in life you keep on stumbling over. You may then compassionately aspire to overcome them. Engage in the positive and do so with all the power of your being. Refrain from the negative proclivities and stay away from them with all the strength of your soul.

HUMANITY

Inclusion and unity is what we seek in our relationships with the Divine, with others, and within ourselves. Unity within begins when we are able to look at ourselves as one unit. We are a composite of utterly transcendent consciousness enclosed within a physical and temporary body that includes a strong sense of ego and identity. Transcendence and unity coupled with total individuation and uniqueness — that's us.

Ego and *Nefesh*, the animating aspect of our soul most closely connected to our physical body, seeks survival. Much like all of created reality, we too are impelled to self-select and survive. As a tree bends towards the light, our bodies naturally are inclined to seek out that which aids perpetuation, whether it is the food our body craves, or the sleep it needs. The body desires self-perpetuation. In fact, it is healthy and adaptive for our growth to be ego based, especially in our younger years of life. Yet, deep within, we sense *Yechida* or unified consciousness. Without thinking people will jump into a fire to save someone else's life, even a person they have never met. On the deepest level we are all aware that the other is part of the I.

Body and soul, or ego and transcendence, while they may appear as divergent or conflicting forces — one constantly seeking unity, while the other tends towards individuation and diversity — are in fact not opposing and they are both to be included within the context of One.

Healthy living is achieved through a balance and alignment of our ego with our sense of transcendence. Life is not about ignoring your self and your needs in order to live like a doormat, nor is it only about satisfying yourself and your desires. You exist and so does the other.

Acknowledge your greatness and then train yourself to see the greatness in others.

Practice looking for the good in others. Remember that the other is a mirror for the One.

Our challenge is not to nullify the ego, as in our sense of selfhood and self-worth, but rather to enlist the ego into the service of our deepest self.

We can either approach life from a purely egocentric point of view, in which case the context is me or you. Or we can come to life from an integrated perspective that is inclusive of me and you. When we operate from the former, one's life becomes a battleground, a clash of egos, between one person and the next or one group and the next.

An un-rectified or un-integrated ego that is walking down the street and is thirsty and then sees a little boy walking to school sipping his milk naturally grabs the milk without even thinking.

This is obviously an extreme example, but it demonstrates a pure 'survival of the fittest' approach to life. Clearly, an ego that is unchecked and unbalanced does not pursue the appropriate means to properly attain its desires. When faced with a choice between its own needs and that of an others, it will rob, steal, cheat, and lie or even worse to fulfill its own needs.

Wherein the ego is self-serving, urging and inspiring us to fulfill our needs and desires in order to secure and sustain our corporeal existence, it is our task to harness and steer our egoic inclination in the direction of a more inclusive paradigm of unity. In this path we seek transparency not nullification. In order to make the ego less opaque and more of an instrument of transcendence, the idea of individuality, with its strong sense of distinction and uniqueness, should be integrated within an over-arching awareness that we are all important parts of a grand cosmic Unity. Each of us is expressing our own uniqueness and thereby expressing another finite facet of the Infinite One.

Ego within transcendence, body within soul — this is a context of me and you. From this place I can sense my selfhood. I can acknowledge that I am unique and have something special to contribute to the world. I can be fully aware that my true potential is articulated when I express myself in the unique way that I think, feel, and function. And yet, I can simultaneously acknowledge that you too are unique and have a particular way of being. I have my genius and you have yours, and together we are both finite expressions of the Infinite One.

GLOSSARY
OF HEBREW WORDS:

Ayin : Emptiness, no-thing-ness. The Unmanifest

Ani or **Anochi** : The Ultimate 'I' of Existence

Atzmut or **Etzem** : The Essence of all Reality.

Chalal : The empty space; the (apparent) void that remains after the *Tzimtzum*

Ein Sof : Literally translates as 'no end'; representing the boundless, formless nature of the Infinite; also understood in the context of *'Ohr Ein Sof'* - limitless Light.

Elokim : Plural G-d name used in the account of creation in Genesis. This name is understood to represent the aspect of G-d that is hidden within nature and the creative process in general.

Hashem: Literally "the Name", what we say instead of the tetragrammaton, the Ineffable, Infinity.

Histalshelut : The cosmic chain of being from Infinite One to finite multiplicity; the archetypal sequence of events that led to Creation; also can be applied to our own inner consciousness and creative processes

Kav :The line/pipe/channel through which the focused and condensed infinite light was able to travel into the structure of the *Sefirot* in order to manifest within the finite realm.

Midrash: Rabbinic writings, often containing 'behind the scenes' stories that fill out the Biblical narrative; part of the oral tradition of Judaism.

Mitzvah *(Mitzvot)* : The commandments from the Torah, also understood as 'Good Deeds', ritual obligations, or actions, that connect us to our highest selves, our community, and Hashem.

Moshe:The Hebrew name of Moses

Rebbe: A Chassidic master.

Sefirot (*Sefira***)** :The 'vessels' or 'lenses' that refract and reflect the infinite light in order that it can manifest in our finite world; a series of cosmic/consciousness transducers that help to transform infinite light into finite form.

Shevirat Hakelim: The cosmic shattering of the vessels.

Shechinah:The Presence of the Creator within the immediacy of creation, the In-dwelling, the Immanent aspect of G-d (also understood as feminine).

Tzimtzum :The cosmic (apparent) withdrawal, contraction of the Infinite Light to make room for finitude.

Talmud : Rabbinic writings that contain *Halacha* (laws), *Aggadah* (legends) and Biblical commentary; part of the oral tradition of the Torah.

Tikkun : Fixing, repairing, or attuning; understood in the context of *'Tikkun Olam'*- to fix, or repair, the world.

Torah : Generally refers to the Bible, the five books of Moses; although in broader definition, this term includes the entire Jewish canon.

Yesh : Something-ness, individual existence (as opposed to the ultimate Existence of Etzem)

Yesh Amiti : Ultimate Existence, True Being, Essence Consciousness

Zohar : Primary multi-volume work of *Kabbalah*, first made public in 1290's.

OTHER BOOKS BY
RAV DOVBER PINSON

IYYUN PUBLISHING

Available in fine book stores everywhere and online at Amazon.com

REINCARNATION AND JUDAISM
The Journey of the Soul

A fascinating analysis of the concept of reincarnation as it appears in the works of the Kabbalistic masters, as well as how it is discussed by the great thinkers throughout history. Dipping into the fountain of ancient wisdom and modern understanding, the book addresses and answers such basic questions as: What is reincarnation? Why does it occur? and How does it affect us personally?

....

INNER RHYTHMS
The Kabbalah of Music

The study of music as response is explored in this highly engaging book. Music and its effects in every aspect of our lives are looked at in the perspective of mystical Judaism and the Kabbalah. The topics range from Deveikut/Oneness, Yichudim/Unifications, merging heaven and earth, to the more personal issues, such as Simcha/Happiness, expressing joy, to the means of utilizing music to medicate the sad soul. Ultimately,using music to inspire genuine transformation.

MEDITATION AND JUDAISM
EXPLORING THE JEWISH MEDITATIVE PATHS

A comprehensive work on Jewish meditation, encompassing the entire spectrum of Jewish thought--from the early Kabbalists to the modern Chassidic and Mussar masters, the sages of the Talmud to the modern philosophers--this book includes them all.

The book is both a scholarly, in-depth study of meditative practices, and a practical, easy to follow guide for any person interested in meditating the Jewish way. The word meditation calls to mind the traditional, obvious associations that society has accumulated, such as the lotus position, the mantras and the like.

Meditation and Judaism attempts to broaden our view of meditation, demonstrating that in addition to the traditional methods of meditation ,meditation is prevalent within so many of the common Jewish practices.

The book also explores a variety of fascinating and intriguing topics such as; panoscopic vision, spiritual synesthesia, psychic powers. What is black magic? What is the Koach HaTumah – the impure powers? What is the definition of spirituality?

TOWARD THE INFINITE
THE WAY OF KABBALISTIC MEDITATION

'Toward the Infinite – A Kabbalistic Meditation' focuses exclusively on the Kabbalistic – Chassidic approach to meditation. Encompassing the entire meditative experience, it takes the reader on a comprehensive and engaging journey through meditation.
The journey begins with the readying of oneself for the meditation. The preparatory stage is discussed at length, dealing with issues such as the time of day most conducive to the meditation, the meditative positions and the like. The journey continues with the actual meditative experience. The various states of consciousness that a person encounters in the course of the meditation, beginning at a level of extreme self-awareness and concluding with a total state of non-awareness.

'Toward the Infinite – A Kabbalistic Meditation' is deliberately written to appeal to a mass audience and thus does not make use of learned quotations and references. An easy read which will pique the interest of all those intrigued by spirituality and meditation.

JEWISH WISDOM OF THE AFTERLIFE
THE MYTHS, THE MYSTERIES & MEANINGS

What happens to us after we physically die? What is consciousness? And can it survive without a physical brain? What is a soul? Can we remember our past lives? Do near-death-experiences prove the immortality of the soul?

Drawing from the fountain of ancient Jewish wisdom and modern understanding of what consciousness is, this book explores the possibilities of surviving death, the near-death-experience, and a possible glimpse of the peace and unconditional love that awaits, empowering the reader to live their day-to-day life with these great spiritual truths.

In 'Jewish Wisdom on the Afterlife', Rav DovBer Pinson explores the possibility of life after death, presenting a basic understanding of what it means to be mortal and how an understanding of our immortality can serve us in the present and empower us to live more meaningfully today.

UPSHERIN
Exploring the Laws, Customs & Meanings of a Boy's First Haircut

What is the meaning of Upsherin, the traditional celebration of a boy's first haircut at the age of three?

This in-depth answer to that question explores as well the questions: Why is a boy's hair allowed to grow freely for his first three years? What is the kabbalistic import of hair in all its lengths and varieties? What is the mystical meaning of hair coverings? Rav DovBer Pinson answers these questions with his trademark deep learning and spiritual sensitivity.

Includes a guide to conducting an Upsherin ceremony.

THIRTY – TWO GATES OF WISDOM:
Awakening through Kabbalah

Kabbalah holds the secrets to a path of conscious awareness. In this compact book, Rav DovBer Pinson presents 32 key concepts of Kabbalah and shows their value in opening the gates of perception.

A short excerpt from the introduction:
Simply translated, Kabbalah means "that which is received." Looking deeper, the word Kabbalah can mean to be open and receptive, to challenge one's own internal navigational system in order to see, hear, and be open to… more. We must be receptive to a teaching to fully absorb it. We turn ourselves into vessels and invite within that which we wish to understand or grasp. In this way, we become receptacles, dispensaries, and a part of the Kabbalah. We become vessels of this tradition by opening the self to a higher reality, and viewing the spirit within the matter. We raise our consciousness to the point where the Divine within all creation is revealed. As we pursue a deeper awareness, we become less ego-centered and more attuned to the deeper significance of our surroundings.

WRAPPED IN MAJESTY: TEFILLIN EXPLORED

In this profound, passionate and thought-provoking text, Rav DovBer Pinson explores and reveals the multi-dimensional perspectives of Tefillin. Rav Pinson magically weaves together all dimensions of Torah;, Peshat, literal observation, to Remez, the allegorical; Derush, the homiletic, to Sod, hidden Kabbalistic, into one wonderful tapestry. Rav Pinson reaches for the underlying unity within all wellsprings of Torah and uncovers the hidden profound mystery of the Tefillin.

THE PURIM READER
The Holiday of Purim Explored

With a Persian name, a costuming dress code and a woman as the heroine, Purim is certainly unusual amongst the Jewish holidays. Most people are very familiar with the costumes, Megillah and revelry, but are mystified by their significance.

Rav DovBer Pinson offers a glimpse into the unknown world of Purim, uncovering the mysteries and offering a deeper understanding of this unique holiday.

EIGHT LIGHTS
8 Meditations for Chanukah

What is the meaning and message of Chanukah? What is the spiritual significance of the Lights of the Menorah? What are the Lights telling us? What is the deeper dimension of the Dreidel?

Rav DovBer Pinson, with his trademark deep learning and spiritual sensitivity guides us through eight meditations relating to the Lights of the Menorah and the eight days of Chanukah, and a deeper exploration of the Dreidel.

Includes a detailed how-to guide for lighting the Chanukah Menorah

THE IYYUN HAGADAH
An Introduction to the Haggadah

In this beautifully written introduction to Passover and the Haggadah, Rav DovBer Pinson, guides us through the major themes of Passover and the Seder night. Rav Pinson addresses the important questions, such as; *What is the big deal of Chametz? What are we trying to achieve through conducting a Seder? What's with all that stuff on the Seder Plate?* And most importantly, *how is this all related to freedom?* His answers will surprise even those who think they already know the answers to these questions.

THE MYSTERY OF KADDISH

The Mystery of Kaddish is an in-depth and Kabbalistic exploration into the Mourner's Kaddish Prayer. Throughout Jewish history, there have been many rites and rituals associated with loss and mourning, yet none have prevailed quite like the Mourner's Kaddish Prayer - which has become the definitive ritual of mourning.

The Mystery of Kaddish explores the source of this prayer and deconstructs the meaning to better understand the grieving process and how the Kaddish prayer supports and uplifts the bereaved through their own personal journey to healing.

RECLAIMING THE SELF
THE WAY OF TESHUVAH

Teshuvah is one of the great gifts of life. It speaks of a hope for a better today and empowers us to choose a brighter tomorrow.

But what exactly is Teshuvah? And how does it work? How can we undo our past and how do we deal with guilt? And what is healthy regret without eroding our self-esteem?

In this fascinating and empowering book, world-renowned teacher and thinker, Rav DovBer Pinson lays out a path for genuine transformation and a way to include all of our past in the powerful moment of the now.

....

PASSPORT TO KABBALAH:
A JOURNEY OF INNER TRANSFORMATION

Life is a journey full of ups and downs, inside-outs, and unexpected detours. There are times when we think we know exactly where we want to be headed, and other times when we are so lost we don't even know where we are.

Rooted in the teachings of Kabbalah, this book provides readers with a passport of sorts to help them through any obstacles along their path of self-refinement, reflection, and self-transformation.

....

THE FOUR SPECIES:
THE SYMBOLISM OF THE LULAV & ESROG

The Arba Minim, or Four Species, have inspired countless commentaries and traditions and intrigued scholars and mystics alike. In this little masterpiece of wisdom - both profound and practical - Rav DovBer Pinson explores the deep symbolic roots and nature of the Four Species

The Na'anuim, or ritual of the Lulav movement, is meticulously detailed and Kavanos, or meditations, are offered for use with the practice. Includes an illustrated guide to the Lulav Movements.